PROVEN WORD BOOKS

- Have *proven* themselves where it counts—among the thousands of readers who have made them best-sellers, who have found these books meaningful in the arena of real life

- Were best-sellers in hardcover and are now made available at more affordable prices in deluxe paperback bindings

- Offer new, built-in study guides with questions to encourage private pondering and group discussion

- Meet the widespread needs of people everywhere who are searching for answers to the pressures and problems of living in the modern world

PROVEN
WORD

THE *Jesus Style*

GAYLE D. ERWIN

Foreword by Richard C. Halverson

PROVEN WORD

WORD PUBLISHING
Dallas · London · Sydney · Singapore

The Jesus Style

Copyright © 1983, 1988 by Gayle D. Erwin

Library of Congress Cataloging in Publication Data

Erwin, Gayle D.
　The Jesus style.

　　Reprint. Originally published: Palm Springs, Calif. R. N. Haynes Publishers, c1983.
　　1. Jesus Christ—Person and offices.　2. Service (Theology)　3. Christian life—1960-　　I. Title.
BT202.E78　1985　　232.9′04　　95-10562
ISBN 0-8499-0509-5
ISBN 0-8499-2989-X (pbk.)

Scripture references, unless otherwise specified, are from the *Holy Bible: New International Version*, Copyright © 1978 by the New York International Bible Society. Used by permission of Zondervan Bible Publishers.

Scripture references, where noted, are from *The Revised Standard Version of the Bible* (RSV), Copyright © 1946, 1952, © 1971 and 1973 by the Division of Christian Education of the National Council of the Churches of Christ in the U.S.A.

Printed in the United States of America

980123 RRD 9876543

To my wife,
Ada,
and my children,
Valerie, Clyde,
Peter and Gloria,
Mark and Angela,
who loved me anyway

For whoever wants to save his life will lose it, but whoever loses his life for me and for the gospel will save it.

(Mark 8:35)

. . . I consider everything a loss compared to the surpassing greatness of knowing Christ Jesus my Lord, for whose sake I have lost all things. I consider them rubbish, that I may gain Christ. . . .

(Philippians 3:8)

Contents

Foreword

The world's first exposure to the Christ was in the human being — the person — the man Jesus. . . the Jewish carpenter turned itinerant rabbi. His teaching was radical, cutting across the religious orthodoxy and the conventional view of the Messiah-King and His kingdom. We fail to hear today what Jesus says since we are always in danger of reading into His radical teaching what we think we already know and believe in our cultural and theological context. Our traditions get in the way.

In *The Jesus Style*, Gayle Erwin helps us to see and feel and hear Jesus as though for the first time without any preconception, predisposition or prejudice. He helps to free us from our traditions and the same dogmatic prison in which the religionists contemporary with Jesus were bound:

And he said to them, "Well did Isaiah prophesy of you hypocrites, as it is written,

'This people honors me with their lips,
but their heart is far from me; in vain
do they worship me, teaching as doc-
trines the precepts of men.'
You leave the commandment of God, and
hold fast the tradition of men." (Mark 7:6-8
RSV)

Some theological scholars have been insisting that
the critical issue in the church is what we believe
about Jesus Christ. In a very basic sense, he has
always been the critical issue in the church and, for
that matter, in history. Invariably and inevitably,
when anything else is made the issue, it tends to
divide those for whom Jesus Christ is Savior and
Lord. One way to look at this is that when other
issues are allowed to polarize those for whom Christ
is Lord, that issue, whatever it is, elevated to a position of greater importance than Christ Himself. One
eminent scholar for whom I have profound admira-
tion and respect put it this way: "Whatever you make
the issue, you make the idol."

That Christ is the critical issue is indisputable. He
made Himself the issue when He confronted the disciples at Caesarea Philippi with the fundamental
question, the answer to which is the foundation upon
which He builds His church:

"But who do you say that I am?" Simon Peter
replied, "You are the Christ, the Son of the
living God." And Jesus answered him,

"Blessed are you, Simon Bar-Jona! For flesh and blood has not revealed this to you, but my Father who is in heaven. (Matthew 16:15-17 RSV)

The apostle John, who wrote his first epistle to those "that believe on the name of the Son of God, was explicit as to the central issue when he defined the criterion for truth:

By this you know the Spirit of God: every spirit which confesses that Jesus Christ has come in the flesh is of God, and every spirit which does not confess Jesus is not of God. (1 John 4:2-3 RSV)

The first heresy in the church did not deny the deity of Jesus, it denied His humanity. Gnosticism, believing matter to be evil, rejected the idea that Christ had a physical body, and affirmed that He only "appeared" to be human. In the first third of this century the controversy about the deity of Jesus dominated the church. In their justifiable preoccupation with the deity of Christ, evangelicals somehow seemed to lose their sense of the humanity of Jesus. In doing so, for all practical purposes, they abandoned the human model which God sent into history to show us, not only what God is like, but humanness as God intended it.

The very essence of the divine strategy, God's consummate revelation of Himself in human flesh, was in effect sacrificed to a dogma which, though absolutely correct, caused us to lose touch with the essential aspect of God's identifying Himself with man.

It is the settled conviction of this writer that this fact is today critical in the evangelical approach to an unbelieving world. Instead of presenting the fascinating, irresistible man Jesus, we communicate a doctrine. The tendency is to ask a person to believe this or that about Christ rather than to know Him, receive Him, trust Him, love Him. Our gospel has become a dogma rather than a fascinating person who was the center and circumference of apostolic faith. The apostles knew very little about Jesus — but they knew Him. We tend, today, to know much about Him — but fail to enjoy an intimate relationship with Him.

The critical issue, then, is Jesus — who He was, what He said and did in His earthly pilgrimage. Gayle Erwin brings us face-to-face with the man Jesus, the real person who walked the dusty roads of Galilee, lived a real life in real situations with real people, and communicated the profoundest truth in the simplest terms.

Out of his own pastoral experience, and early failures it might be added, the author forces his readers to consider honestly, or perhaps it is even better to say reconsider, the simple teaching of Jesus with which they are already very familiar. In this book we are presented with the Jesus of the New Testament in a way which penetrates our traditional views and demands that we abandon the rationalizations we have invented which allow us to profess to be Jesus' disciples while at the same time giving Him half-hearted, partial obedience.

Personally, I met Jesus in a new way reading this book, for which I am deeply grateful.

In reading, I thought of John's opening statement in his first epistle, "That which was from the beginning, which we have heard, which we have seen with our eyes, which we have looked upon and touched with our hands, concerning the word of life. . . that which we have seen and heard we proclaim also to you. . ." (1 John 1:1, 3 RSV)

RICHARD C. HALVERSON
Chaplain, United States Senate

Preface

This book was born out of a crisis of understanding and purpose that occurred in my life during an early pastorate. At that time, I did not know how far-reaching the effects of that crisis would be. There came a point in which simple integrity demanded that I begin to match my pastoral activities to what I understood the Bible to teach, rather than permit tradition and cultural expectations to rule my actions. I discovered, however, that the bridge between the real and the ideal seems to be in disrepair — you cross at your own risk and you dare not carry excess baggage from your past habits.

Crossing that bridge becomes a source of disillusionment with much of the familiar and skirts dangerously close to a chasm of apathetic cynicism. I have often wished I could ask God one specific question and know that he would answer it fully for me: "Why have you let your church get in such dismal shape with factions, fightings and heresies?" I don't have that answer, but I have come to an understanding of principle and purpose that has rescued me and, in my view, has the potential of freeing the church to become what Jesus designed it to be.

A Style of His Own

Jesus—Yes

It was only one of the many placards we saw wielded by the protestors of the sixties, but it arrested me. The sign simply said, "Jesus — yes! Christianity — no!"

I pondered, "Why, through all these years, has the reality of Jesus remained innately attractive while our interpretations of him have proved less captivating?" Somewhere we have missed an understanding of him that portrays him properly. But, what? Could there be anything about him that we have not researched or developed? Is there a key? I share my search with you.

The focal point of all time, all history, all study (my bias is evident) is the person of Jesus Christ. Yet, this book is not about the omniscience, omnipotence or omnipresence of Jesus, not about predestination or the foreknowledge of God. These traits, as I read them in systematic theologies and

1

their treatment of his nature, place Jesus beyond my reach — sometimes, I think, safely so. What more can be said of his visual awesomeness than the word pictures in the first chapter of Revelation?

Instead of these overwhelming, majestic descriptions with endless possibilities of theological convolutions, I want to speak of his incarnation. I want to take his thundering power, compress it into the body that was his, place your hand against his skin and, if your mind can handle it (I know that your spirit can), let you know that the touch and the warmth you feel is God himself.

When that first cry was heard from the stable of Bethlehem and into the care of Mary and Joseph came a wrinkled, blood-covered baby, the universe reached its turning point. For the first time, the God and Creator who before had been only heard could now be seen and touched. All that he was now occupied human flesh . . . approachable, available, vulnerable. Yet, mankind prefers the unseen, distant God. We have difficulty with the God who is living flesh. We would rather wrestle with principles, dogmas and ideas than hear him call us to himself as a person.

But God would not have it that way. Jesus, the dividing point of time, could be touched, and he put us in touch with God. It is appropriate that the records show him going everywhere touching people, even those who had been untouchable until that time. Ironically, the records also show that those he touched did not understand who he was. Even his closest followers were often uncertain.

The Upside Down Kingdom

John the Baptist, Jesus own cousin, is an example of that uncertainty. Early in his ministry he said of Jesus: "This is the one!" Later, he asked, speaking out of his doubts, "Are you the one?"

What happened in the meantime? Why did he get confused about who Jesus actually was? John gives us a clue to what might have been the source of his confusion. At the time he made the first statement, he revealed that he would not have known Jesus had it not been for the Spirit descending and remaining on him. In other words, there was nothing automatically messianic in his appearance (a difficult thing to believe when we look at the artistic portrayals of Jesus) nor did his actions match the traditional expectations of the Messiah.

Though John preached the message of preparation given to him, he, along with the disciples who were constantly asking Jesus when he was going to throw off Rome and establish the kingdom, may well have harbored a traditional understanding of the Messiah. Somehow, whatever their expectations, Jesus did not coincide with their, or our, popular understandings of the Messiah. The question is, "How do we align our understanding with the truth?"

The disciples repeatedly struggled with what Jesus was trying to teach them about the kingdom of God. They jockeyed for position, maneuvered for favor, argued over who was the greatest. I, frankly, appreciate seeing their humanness. Naturally, I consider myself too sophisticated today to stoop to such a crass approach. Instead, when I go into committee meetings, I scheme about how I can get the others to do what I want them to do while they think it is what they want to do and then, ultimately, to give me the credit for it. Or I join with others in clever political maneuverings behind the scenes at church conventions and remain conveniently blind to my own motivation.

Jesus responded clearly and firmly to the competitive discussions of the disciples (and to my own motives):

> "You know that those who are regarded as rulers of the Gentiles lord it over them, and their high officials exercise authority over them. Not so with you. Instead, whoever wants to become great among you must be your servant, and whoever wants to be first must be slave of all. For even the Son of Man did not come to be served, but to serve, and to give his life as a ransom for many." (Mark 10:42-45)

This man said he came to serve rather than be served. He rules, as one author put it, in an "upside down kingdom." As we study him, we may be in for as many surprises as were the disciples. When John the Baptist asked, "Are you the one?" Jesus responded by listing his caring, healing actions — actions somewhat less dramatic than the traditional expectations of the Messiah. John was still in jail, undelivered. Rome was still in control. Where was Jesus the king? Either something had gone wrong or the misunderstanding had been complete. Jesus, knowing the tension between his reality and our understanding, stated: "Blessed is the man who does not fall away on account of me" (Luke 7:23).

This is the Jesus I want to talk about, the Jesus who called himself a servant. For reasons I cannot understand, I have not, in my research, found the qualities of servanthood, which seem so self-evident and basic to who Jesus is, treated in any but a surface and brief way. I only know that the realization of them and even minimal incorporation of them into life has power that I cannot describe; I can only invite you to it.

We will look at these characteristics in the following chapter.

The Jesus Approach

Let's pose a speculative question. What if you were God and wished to completely reveal yourself to a planet? Knowing the awesome disparity between yourself and the people of that planet, what would be your first act?

There is no end of irony and incongruity in the way God did choose to reveal himself. Let's look at some of the paradoxical events that happened when Jesus entered our world.

Born in a Barn

What an unlikely place for a king to be born! After a difficult journey for a woman in the ninth month of pregnancy, a stable is the last place that a caring husband would want her to be. The Nativity scenes that decorate the landscape during Christmas season are something less than accurate. None of them smell quite right. We don't fully understand the unsanitary conditions of having to walk carefully around the droppings of animals and then lay a newborn baby, fresh from the pains of delivery, in a feeding trough streaked with the saliva of animals.

We don't fully understand the embarrassment Joseph must have felt to watch his wife go through this pain in these surroundings. The Son of God deserved something better.

My four children were all born under very sanitary conditions — so sanitary that I was unwelcome. It was somewhat devastating as a father to have the nurses quickly remove the newborn baby from the mother's room because I was coming in.

If God would have consulted with me, since I have had some experience in public relations, I would have advised him to snap his fingers and create a multistory, magnificently modern hospital gleaming bright on the outside with a giant diamond on the top to catch the sun's rays and scatter them over the countryside. His Son, of course, would be the exclusive user. All the world could then visit and gasp in wonder at the birthplace of the Son of God.

But he didn't consult with me and instead had his Son born in a barn. This was a birth that could impress no one, and certainly no one would be threatened by it. Most could even brag about their better circumstances. Maybe we can cheer for his city. Or can we?

And how about his choice of location? A famous city would have increased people's ability to remember him and definitely would have improved his image. But Bethlehem? There are not sufficient hotels and motels and convention centers to make this an appropriate place to visit and honor the memory of the King. No, Bethlehem was not large enough to warrant having the Son of God born there. But he was. No one could be intimidated by his birthplace. Ah, but royalty is royalty and the sophistication of his parentage will show through. Or will it?

And what about his parentage? We believe in the virgin birth now. This doctrine has been deliberated upon and agreed to by most of the Christian world. However, at the time of Jesus' birth they did not know about the virgin birth. Jesus grew up amidst whispers of "bastard" and the stigma of having been conceived out of wedlock.

What if the choice young girl of an outstanding church youth group suddenly appeared pregnant? Nothing about her life would indicate that such would ever happen, so everyone is shocked. With great hesitation and embarrassment, the leader of the group finally gets up enough courage to ask her who the father is. She responds, "The Holy Spirit." The church would laugh her to scorn.

Do you suppose the friends and neighbors of

Jesus never asked him why he didn't favor Joseph? Do you suppose his childhood friends never gathered and laughed at his claim that the Holy Spirit was his father? Do you suppose the Pharisees never brought it up to him?

In biblical times a bastard and his descendants to the tenth generation were excluded from the assembly of the Lord. Bastards had no claim to paternal care or the usual privileges and discipline of legitimate children. Though we know that is not what Jesus was, the world viewed him differently. If you were seeking to be recognized as God, you wouldn't want this sort of thing on your record. Any opponents would have buckets of mud to sling in your face. The whispering campaign would be devastating. But multitudes of people who had borne the taunts of the world would now find one whose birth wouldn't intimidate them, one who could redeem them. How utterly vulnerable he made himself to the caustic world. Born of a virgin. And, if that wasn't enough, his ancestry left him with few bragging points.

His Family's Checkered Past

Genealogies have never inspired me, and, from what I hear, many people have tired of reading the Bible once they had to wade through the begats. But there is more to the record of Christ's ancestry than a list of names. Just as a study of our own heritage may produce a horse thief or two, Jesus, were he not "God with us," would be embarrassed by some from whom he issued.

The beloved purity of the Jewish line was compromised in Ruth the Moabite and Rahab the Canaanite. Further shame! Rahab was a prostitute. Jacob, as his name indicated, was a noted cheat. Judah was a womanizer. David, on whose throne Christ sits and whose name he takes, was an adulterer and murderer whose bloodstained hands precluded his building the temple. Out of David's union with Bathsheba, for whom he murdered Uriah, comes Solomon, who, in spite of his wisdom, had hundreds of wives and concubines and turned his heart away from God.

We may be proud of royal or outstanding genetic strains in our ancestry, but this amazing Jesus foregoes such a luxury so that his ancestry can never intimidate us and the skeptic can never claim that he was merely the final product of a super race.

Jesus also managed his messiahship without the privilege of an unusual name. You may protest that the name of Jesus is not a common name and definitely not a weak one. But we need to understand its background before we jump to those conclusions.

To begin with, his name was not actually Jesus. His name was Joshua. It was a good name, meaning "Jehovah is salvation"; but it was a very common name — not one appropriate to a king.

The name Joshua comes to us through the Greek

as Jesus. We have used it that way unquestioningly. It is easy to understand the change when
we see how the name James translates into Spanish
as either Iago or Jaime.

Because the common name of Joshua did not
stand out from all the rest it is a clue to his nature
for he was also to be called Immanuel — which
means "God with us." He chose to identify himself
with his people, not stand apart from them.

What name would we recommend for him if
we were to suggest one more appropriate for a
king? Wouldn't we want a smooth sounding, attractive, looks-good-in-lights, unique, Hollywood
stage name? But Joshua? There were probably
three in his block already. Why even bother to
announce a birth that is off to such a bad start?
And the way it was handled, it would have to
be considered a rather weak announcement.

Again you may protest. "Wait a minute. They
didn't have angels singing when I was born. How
can you call that a weak announcement?" You
will see.

The Way He Arrived

First, if God would have consulted with me, I
would have recommended that he make the announcement with a little more flair. Perhaps he
should stand on the moon with an expensive mi-
crophone, hang two billion-watt speakers out in

space and then broadcast: "Hello-o-o-o-o, Wo-o-o-rld. This is Go-o-o-o-d."

Or, since God chose to go with a choir, I would have recommended that he follow the chain of command and go to the Sanhedrin first or at least use his energies wisely and go to the marketplace and get the announcement to the greatest number of people in the shortest time.

But no, he persists in picking a desolate spot. What if you had been one of the members of that angelic choir chosen to announce the birth? For 200 years you have been practicing and anticipating the glorious presentation. Everything is in perfect tune and timing for the concert of the ages. For 100 years they have been building a stage in the sky for that great moment.

Then Gabriel says, "He's born! You're on, fellows!" The curtains are pulled back and you see the crowd — six shepherds!? What a letdown! "Okay," someone asks, "who was in charge of posters?"

Shepherds weren't exactly in the centers of communication. Their captive audience could only talk to other sheep. Also, shepherds were not the best messengers to be carrying such important news. In the time of Jesus, they had lost the respectful reputation that they might have had in the time of David. Now, they were a group with a questionable reputation. They tended to be a little light fingered with other people's property. Nor were they particularly welcome in town. People didn't put much stock in their word either.

Can you hear the conversation in a home in Bethlehem? The shepherds have visited the manger and then leave town knocking on doors as they go, all the while yelling, "Joshua is born! Joshua is born!"

"Oh boy! another Joshua in this neighborhood. That's all we need. Who said that, anyway?"

"Oh, just our friendly local burglar."

"What did you say?"

As we read about this primitive birth announcement, we are amazed at who gets elevated in the presence of the servant, Jesus. Anyway, wait until we see his face, then we will be properly awed . . won't we?

The Way He Looked

Jesus was not handsome. This you may find difficult to accept. You might respond, "Now you have gone too far. I have his picture on my wall and he isn't ugly. He is striking — a really fine figure of a man." Sorry, but Isaiah tells us how he looked:

> He had no beauty or majesty to attract
> us to him,
> nothing in his appearance that we
> should desire him.
> Isaiah 53:2

Jesus was so common in his looks that often he was able to lose himself in crowds. Judas had to identify him with a kiss, even after three years in the public eye. Who knows — the traitor may have been better-looking than the betrayed?

This is a good clue to Jesus' approach to persons. I know how I feel when I am in the presence of inordinately handsome men — jealous!

But Jesus came in a form that was not intimidating to anyone. All could feel at ease around him. His looks in no way separated him from the common, poor people to whom he was sent. But if his face didn't separate him, surely his home would, wouldn't it? Let's look at that aspect of his coming.

Have you ever wondered what you would have done if the Messiah had been born into your family? Here you have the most precious jewel in all of history. Now what are you going to do with him? What kind of home would you buy? What kind of city would you choose? What kind of neighborhood would you select? What kind of friends would you permit him to have? Some things are so valuable that you don't know what to do with them. You would not carry the Hope diamond around in your pocket or wear it on a chain around your neck in public places.

Can Anything Good Come Out of Nazareth?

But Joseph and Mary now had the Son of God in their possession. What were they to do? They took him to Nazareth (after fleeing for their lives to Egypt). But surely Nazareth was not the place to raise the Son of God. The moral and religious reputation of Nazareth was so bad that Nathaniel's response to meeting Jesus of Nazareth was: "Can anything good come out of Nazareth?" (John 1:47).

So Jesus consistently found himself moving among and identifying with the least in life. But his Father owns the cattle on a thousand hills. Let's see what happens when he starts spending that money.

Ownership of things is central to Western society. As I tour through the Beverly Hills section of Hollywood in California, I am dutifully impressed with the displays of wealth — massive homes, automobiles, security guards. The owners' importance is evident.

But Jesus never owned more than what he carried on his back. No one could be very impressed or intimidated by that. He said of himself: "Foxes have holes and birds of the air have nests, but the Son of Man has no place to lay his head" (Matthew 8:20).

How does he expect to impress this economic world without even a house to sleep in? He simply didn't view riches the same way we do. In the Sermon on the Mount, his words were straightforward:

> "Do not store up for yourselves treasures on earth, where moth and rust destroy, and where thieves break in and steal. But store up for yourselves treasures in heaven, where moth and rust do not destroy, and

where thieves do not break in and steal.
For where your treasure is, there your heart
will be also." (Matthew 6:19-21)

Jesus was not fooled by money. It was not important to him. He who was able to pay taxes
from coins found in the mouth of a fish and turn
stones to bread could easily have been the financial
baron of all times.

The problem with wealth, however, is that it
affects our relationships with people. If I know
people are wealthy, I have a difficult time being
real around them. I become much too "nice." (After all, you never know when you might want
to borrow from them.)

Jesus' decision to remain uninvolved with the
world's goods freed him from the hidden agenda
of jealousy that would affect any conversation
with someone more wealthy, or less wealthy, than
he. Thus he was able to direct all of his energies
and sensitivity toward the real needs of the persons to whom he was ministering and he was able
to act out of love alone.

Paul, in 2 Corinthians 8:9, wrote that "though
he was rich, yet for your sakes he became poor,
that you through his poverty might become rich."
Jesus, by choosing to walk this earth unencum-
bered by riches, was choosing not to let anything
come in the way of his giving himself to people.
He had not come to redeem things. He had come
to redeem people. And he gave himself fully to
us.

And he came with a very strange advance man.

If I were organizing a series of crusades around my own ministry and sending someone ahead to prepare the way, I would send a handsome, smartly dressed, smooth talking ambassador who would in no way embarrass me. Jesus obviously didn't do it my way. Instead, he used a raving, rough-hewn man who dressed inappropriately for a minister and was committed to organic foods. To top it all, he closed his services by doing a most undignified thing — dunking in water those who were brave enough to respond:

> And so John came, baptizing in the desert region and preaching repentance and baptism for the forgiveness of sins. John wore clothing made of camel's hair, with a leather belt around his waist, and he ate locusts and wild honey. (Mark 1:4,6)
> John said to the crowds coming out to be baptized by him, "You brood of vipers! Who warned you to flee from the coming wrath?" (Luke 3:7)

How tactless can you be? If I were Jesus, I would be afraid I would have to spend most of my time explaining the actions of my forerunner. However, Jesus' whole life was marked by the use of the most unlikely persons. He always saw people differently than I do. That view of people becomes obvious when we look at some of his other choices.

His Motley Crew

When we get a new president in the United States, everyone watches closely to see who he surrounds himself with — what kind of staff and cabinet he chooses. So the Son of God comes to earth and begins to reveal what kind of "reign" he will have by putting together his traveling band of people.

Now, I would have told him to go to the best known seminary and pick at least three professors who have a good grasp on theology and all its ramifications. Then he should go to Hollywood and get people with "charisma" who can command the attention of the crowds and explain to them what he meant when he said something. Then go to Wall Street and pick a few millionaires. (It's always good to have a few of them on the team.) Then, by all means, go to Muscle Beach and pick six bodyguards, otherwise those religious leaders might have him crucified.

But, Jesus didn't check with me. Instead, he went to the streets and wharves and picked out the strangest crew ever to be sent out on a mission to change the world. Had you been walking within fifty feet of them you probably would have detected the odor of fish. He had a Zealot and a tax collector on the team. (This is a combination not unlike a Black revolutionary and a Ku Klux Klan member.) Some of them had heavily identifiable accents inappropriate to the need for eloquence on the team. Jesus was found constantly among the sordid — from the violent to the crafty to the sensual.

I would have fired Peter within a week or two of his hiring. His life indicates that he suffered from foot-in-mouth disease. His impulsiveness decreased his usefulness to fifty percent at the most. Yet Jesus let him remain and even gave him prominence. How could that be unless Jesus sees people far differently than I do and patiently calls the best from them?

I find the analysis of his crew very encouraging. If he could work with them, then he can work with me . . . and you. He doesn't use the criteria that we naturally would. A want ad calling for the weary and heavy laden was hardly the way to pull together the most skilled of followers. And he continues to call the unlikely:

> Brothers, think of what you were when you were called. Not many of you were wise by human standards; not many were influential; not many were of noble birth. But God chose the foolish things of the world to shame the wise; God chose the weak things of the world to shame the strong . . . so that no man may boast before him. (1 Corinthians 1:26-27, 29)

His love for and view of persons is beyond the limit of my logic, but they are very much compatible with his nature.

The only thing left that could have saved his reputation was a rapid and overwhelming rescue from death. But, I'm afraid that his death was the final blow to any chance for impressiveness. Let's look at what happened.

The Way He Died

We would all agree that Jesus died a notorious death, yet I found that I didn't understand the extent of his shame. The truth of scriptural description was lost on me: "For the message of the cross is foolishness to those who are perishing. . ." (1 Corinthians 1:18). The cross was never foolishness to me. I saw it everywhere. It gracefully adorned lofty steeples. In polished silver or burnished wood, it decorated the interiors of churches and other religious buildings. It hung in expensive jewelry around elegant necks. It graced the lapels of suits and marked the fancy stationery of big churches. It was sung about and proclaimed. People carried huge and heavy crosses for penance or publicity. The cross permeated my world. But it was never foolishness. How could it be?

Then it occurred to me that I didn't truly understand the cross, primarily because people don't die on crosses in these days. Had Jesus come to this age, we would have treated him far more humanely. We would have electrocuted him or hanged him or gassed him or placed him before the firing squad or at least injected him with a lethal dose of drugs.

Imagine the results of such a modern execution. I would now be collaring people on the streets and witnessing in this manner: "Neighbor, my best friend just died in the electric chair for you. If you will believe this and take up your electric chair and follow him, you will be saved." Our great hymns would certainly be different. Can you hear us singing, "At the electric chair, at the electric chair, where I first saw the light"? Or, "There's room in the gas chamber for you"? Or, "Take up your firing squad and follow me"?

We would become the laughing stock of the world. We would be embarrassed that our "hope" had died so shamefully, even though we knew he had been resurrected. Such a death is really tough on our image of the cross. Let us paraphrase the Scripture and see how it sounds.

"Jews demand miraculous signs and Greeks look for wisdom, but we preach Joshua electrocuted: a stumbling block to Jews and foolishness to Gentiles . . ." (1 Corinthians 1:22-23 — with apologies).

"For I resolved to know nothing while I was with you except Joshua Messiah and him electrocuted" (1 Corinthians 2:2 — with apologies).

If I were to identify with someone in their death, I would want it to be a heroic death worthy of medals of honor rather than the death of a common criminal. His "cup" was more than mere death, it was the shameful, degrading sentence that comes from carrying the sins, the crimes, the atrocities of all creation on his shoulders.

Now, let's look back to see what we have discovered.

The Chance to Choose

When I look at the clues we have discussed that indicate the nature of Jesus — born in a barn, questionable parents, spotty ancestry, common name, misdirected announcement, unattractive looks, reared in a bad neighborhood, owning nothing, surrounding himself with unattractive co-workers, and dying a shameful death — I find his whole approach unable to fit into the methods that automatically come to mind when I think about "winning the world."

His whole approach could easily be described as nonthreatening or nonmanipulative. He seemed to lead with weakness in each step of life. He had nothing in the world and everything in God and the Spirit.

With this kind of approach to us, he could be sure that our response would be an honest one. None of the methods that would coerce us and get something less than genuine belief were used. This is indicative of true love. Being an others-oriented person, a servant to others, made him want to free them to be as real and honest as possible. He wanted them to be able to make genuine decisions.

On Thanksgiving Day of 1956, I shivered more from fear and excitement than I did from the biting cold of Memphis, Tennessee as I held a ring in my hand and asked Ada Faye Brown to become my wife. Fortunately, she agreed. I could have done it another way. I could have held a ring in one hand and a pistol in the other hand and told her that she was going to marry me for her own good. Had it happened that way, every meal she fixed for me I would have made the dog taste first to see if he remained alive. Love only wants a genuine response.

We make so few genuine decisions in life. Most of the choices we make are affected by outside forces and demands. But when it comes to the most important decision in life — our decision about God — Jesus seeks only a genuine one. So, we are approached in a way that lovingly frees us to make that decision genuinely. We can accept or reject. God refuses to violate our personhood and our power to choose. That is love.

The Style Setter

Number One

If one were to objectively examine the Bible and try to list events and persons in some sort of priority, Jesus becomes without question the central figure. Jesus himself said: "I am the way and the truth and the life. No one comes to the Father except through me. If you really knew me, you would know my Father as well. From now on, you do know him and have seen him" (John 14:6-7).

The Holy Spirit helped Paul to see Jesus as recorded in his letter to the Colossians:

He is the image of the invisible God, the firstborn over all creation. For by him all things were created: things in heaven and on earth, visible and invisible, whether thrones or powers or rulers or authorities; all things were created by him and for him. He is before all things, and in him all things hold together. And he is the head of the body, the church; he is the beginning and the firstborn from among the dead, so that in everything he might have the supremacy. For God was pleased to have all his fullness dwell in him, and through him to reconcile to himself all things. (Colossians 1:15-20)

Since Jesus is everything that God is but expressed in bodily form and since all the treasures of wisdom and knowledge are in him, we can each say:

If I am to know God, I will know him through Jesus.
If I am to gain knowledge, it is deposited in Jesus.
If I am to have wisdom, I will find it in Jesus.
If God dwells in me, it is because Jesus dwells in me.
If I wish to study God, I must study Jesus.
If the Holy Spirit is active in my life, I will hear him speak of Jesus.

His personality, his life and his words are to be grasped and assimilated with all our energy. In everything he must have supremacy. However, I must confess that other things have found a more sure place in my life. Far too much of my thought life is centered in the things that appear to provide security — acquisition of funds and titles, realization of ambitions, for instance. Perhaps these have gained prominence because of my faulty view of the reality of Jesus. Spiritual myopia tends to distort my vision. Anything that "works" or "prospers" (as I culturally understand prosperity) and has his name attached to it does so (I often conclude) because I am doing it the Jesus way, and therefore, he is blessing it. So, many "successful" worldly systems of operation I uncritically accept as God-inspired simply because they cloak themselves with the name of Jesus or the form of a church.

But to realize my failing is not necessarily to understand and follow the answer. How do I correct this faulty view? Must I truly live the nature of Jesus? For an answer, let us look at a command that he gives and emphasizes, literally demanding that the disciples conform to it.

One for All

Jesus gave many commands to the disciples and all those who would follow him, but all of them are mere subheads to the primary command he left us: "A new commandment I give you: Love one another. As I have loved you, so you must love one another. All men will know that you are my disciples if you love one another" (John 13:34,35).

Two things grab my attention immediately as I read this. First, Jesus has authorized only one identifying mark of his followers, love for one another. Not my knowledge of Scripture. Not my style of clothing nor its percentage of body coverage. Not the rituals I go through each week. Not my membership in a specific organization. Not my hair length or other adornment. Not even my orthodoxy. Only my love for others properly brands me.

Saying this brings immediate protest to my mind.

It sounds as if Christ is negating the necessity of knowledge, of holy living, of proper looks by saying only those who love are his. He doesn't even mention the proper routing of spiritual experience and practice in this context. What about conviction, salvation, sanctification, baptism, holy living, tithing? Are these not labels? Won't they identify me just as quickly? In our minds they might, but Jesus certainly doesn't give them any credence here. Is this a cheap and easy gospel he is finally dishing out to us? Hardly! It does not take long for me to realize that I am a hopelessly selfish, unloving person (with notable, but inconsistent exceptions) without the presence and power of Christ within me.

The second item of attention was his command to love each other "as I have loved you." I knew there was a catch somewhere. Does this mean we are all going to have to be crucified just like he was, else we will not love as he did? Frankly, I find that possibility unattractive and very impractical. If all the Christians get themselves crucified, who will spread the gospel? This could give rise to an interesting new church ritual. But wait! When Jesus gave this remarkable command to his disciples, he had not yet been crucified, and they still seemed to understand what he meant. Not even Peter asked the question, "What do you mean by *love*?" Something about Jesus' total actions toward them up to this time had not only convinced them of his love for them but also laid down a practical, imitable pattern.

In our culture, if we wish someone to know that we love them, we merely say "I love you." Although he may have done so, there is no evidence in Scripture that Jesus employed such means. I doubt that he lined the disciples up and said, "Peter, I love you. James, I love you. John, I love you. Judas, I uh . . ."

Jesus' servanthood to the disciples made his love clear. No one had ever loved them in this wholly unselfish way. So important is this command and example that, once you see it clearly, you will discover it to be the common thread that weaves the New Testament together

All for One

Few themes are clearer in the New Testament than that of love. Jesus himself underscores its prominence:

> One of them, an expert in the law, tested him with this question: "Teacher, which is the greatest commandment in the Law?" Jesus replied: " 'Love the Lord your God with all your heart, with all your soul and with all your mind. This is the first and greatest commandment. And the second is like it: 'Love your neighbor as yourself.' All the Law and the Prophets hang on these two commandments." (Matthew 22:35-40)

In other words, "This is what the Bible is all about." Incredible! With this much prominence for love of God and love of one's neighbor, it came as a shock to me to find out that such a statement was missing from the great doctrinal statements of denominations, missing from the great systematic theologies, missing from the creedal statements, and, most unfortunate, missing from our daily lives.

But still, does this servanthood nature of Jesus fulfill all the elements of Jesus' love? And what are the things that love will do? The apostle Paul makes a classic statement about love in 1 Corinthinians 13. Here he tells us that glossolalia and eloquence, prophecy and knowledge, faith and philanthropy are all worthless without love. That hits us at our weakest points. The speaking circuit is most easily opened to the eloquent who can move us and to those who can excite us with the possibility of speaking with the tongues of angels, but Paul denounces these "dynamic" speakers if they are loveless. Periodically, prophetic students hit the trail to reveal to us times, seasons, dates or to give us the latest word direct from God. Our hunger causes us to welcome them with open arms, but Paul again relegates this to dust if it is without love.

I teach in a college. There, knowledge is the premium. It is the only thing we know how to grade, and it is the only thing that will ultimately bring the reward of a degree. Persons of such knowledge and degree are held up for example in our institution and in others, yet Paul equates it with mindlessness if love is not the guiding force.

Faith and faith teaching is big business in Christian circles. If a practitioner were to come along and state that he was going to move Pike's Peak from Colorado to Nebraska and then do it, every news medium in the country would follow him relentlessly, and he would be in highest demand to speak in the largest auditoriums. Demonstrated faith is a big producer, but Paul reduces it to paganism if it is not motivated by love.

The world gladly accepts the efforts of a philanthropist, especially one who is so generous that he is even willing to have slave marks burnt into his body, thereby belonging to someone else. But, strangely enough, even that can be motivated by something other than love and become meaningless. Some giving is done for influence or for tax benefit.

Eloquence, faith, knowledge, giving are all good in our eyes and beneficial, but it is love that is the height of achievement. Even the good and beneficial become deliverers of death if they are not motivated by love.

Paul goes on to give a powerful, overwhelming list of what love is and does:

Love is patient
Love is kind
Love does not envy
Love does not boast
Love is not proud
Love is not rude
Love is not self-seeking
Love is not easily angered
Love keeps no record of wrongs
Love does not delight in evil

Love rejoices in the truth
Love always protects
Love always trusts
Love always hopes
Love always perseveres
Love never fails

Servanthood fulfills these actions by its very nature. Listen, also, to the demand for love in the letters of John:

This is how we know what love is: Jesus Christ laid down his life for us. And we ought to lay down our lives for our brothers. If anyone has material possessions and sees his brother in need but has no pity on him, how can the love of God be in him? Dear children, let us not love with words or tongue but with actions and in truth. (1 John 3:16-18)

When I was struck with the fact that our relationship with God and our effectiveness in the world is predicated on our ability to love one another, I began to see that there was a wealth of instruction about how we are to treat "one another" in the New Testament. Here is a sampling:

Kindly affectioned one to another
In honor preferring one another
Of the same mind one to another
Not judging one another·
Following peace and edifying one another

Receiving one another
Admonishing one another
Saluting one another with a holy kiss
Having the same care one for another
Serving one another
Forbearing one another
Being kind and tenderhearted one to another
Forgiving one another
Submitting one to another
Not lying one to another
Comforting one another
Edifying one another
Being impartial one to another
Wait for one another
Pray for one another
Love one another (many times)

Here again, servanthood fulfills these commands by nature, by very definition. Years ago, I heard a speaker at an Easter sunrise service state that the Bible has much to say about what to believe but little to say about how we are to relate to people. Nothing could be further from the truth! It is time that we took this abundant store of instruction and developed a theology of relationships. With this we might be better able to live as citizens of the kingdom of God. With this understanding of relationships we may see more clearly the principles of Scripture in their proper perspective. With this we may be less abusive of Scripture for selfish gain.

Every year, in classes that introduce students to the principles of Christian education, I have asked them to write a brief paper about the teacher who most affected their life and had most motivated them to learn. Without exception, these have been teachers who loved them and exhibited that love. Expertise in the subject and refinement in teaching method was secondary to the power of love. However, no educational institution that I know of chooses its faculty on the basis of their ability to love, including institutes of biblical learning.

This case for the necessity of love and the necessity to love as Jesus loved is certainly not exhaustive. Hopefully, it will be clear that the servant nature of Jesus answers all the questions we have of love.

One of Many

The great high priestly prayer of Jesus recorded in the seventeenth chapter of the Gospel of John can only be understood in the context of his prior commandment to love one another. By his great commandment in chapter thirteen, he has made it clear that our relationship with God is evidenced by our relationship with each other. Now, in his prayer, he reveals that the evangelistic side of the relationship coin is also bound up in my ability to love my brother.

Five times in this great prayer, Jesus prays for the same thing — a repetition that should catch our attention. For his followers he prays that they being many may be made one. His prayer is amazingly simple. He prays that we may be one just as he and the Father are one! I must admit that though I am a believer in the Trinity, I do not understand it. It is difficult for me to understand how three separate and distinct persons can be one inseparable God without being a committee — a committee that perhaps voted two to one to send Jesus to the earth. Yet their unity was such that Jesus was able to say, "Anyone who has seen me has seen the Father." What kind of unity must we have in order to say, "If you want to know what kind of Christian I am, just check another Christian out . . . I am like him"? For this to occur, there must be change and improvement in the kind of love we are expressing to each other within and across denominational lines.

Another expression that he connects with his prayer for unity has serious implications for evangelism. He prayed, "May they be brought to complete unity *to let the world know that you sent me* and have loved them even as you have loved me" (John 17:23 — italics mine). Most of my evangelistic efforts have revolved around developing even more creative means to get the Gospel past the defenses of the world. So I have moved into better sales systems for personal soul winning, into better staging of programs for auditoriums, into more eloquent speakers, into more dramatic use of the media. Yet the power source for effectively winning the world lies in how well we love one another and effect the unity that Jesus prays for. Why should the world listen to us until they see that fruit which most properly indicates our abiding in Christ? Until the fruit of unity is evident, Christianity is merely another philosophical system to be debated but not to be lived. Surely we can see that selfishness is the source of division and servanthood is the basis of unity. If true love were seen among us, the world might even begin to beat a path to our door and "take the kingdom by force."

In his command in John 13 and in his prayer in John 17, Jesus holds his followers up for judgment by the world — "all men will know that you are my disciples" and "to let the world know that you sent me." Here again my mind protests. It seems unfair! Most of my life I have hidden behind the rationalization that "You can't judge me; you only see the outside, but God sees my heart." That may be true, yet God has here authorized the world to check our fruit of salvation and growth.

I have a tree in my yard that I was told, when I purchased the house, was a peach tree. True, it is shaped like a peach tree and has leaves similar to a peach tree, but in all these years it has never borne a peach. When I decide to approach that tree with an axe so that it will no more encumber the ground, it may plead with me, "Don't cut me down. You can't judge me by the outside. In my heart I am really a peach tree." Such pleas will be unheeded. It was created and planted for fruit, not for peach hearts!

The question I must ask myself is whether I am part of the fulfillment of this prayer of Jesus. Am I a gate to his kingdom or am I a lock on the door that will not let anyone in unless they know the right combination — my combination, of course?

Here again, I am faced with the necessity to love and serve others — first to be identified as a Christian and second to be effective in winning the world. So, what does the evidence say? If I am to love as Jesus commanded and be in unity with the body as he requested, I must know that he is the full revelation of the Father and is my example. If I am filled with the Holy Spirit, I must hear him speak of Jesus and follow the guidance of the Spirit in being like Jesus.

The Jesus Style

Within Our Reach

No theology is of any threat or consequence until we try to apply it to our lives. Such is the case with this study of Jesus. Our lives will be safely humdrum until we dare to live like our master. At that point we can expect this promise of Jesus to come true: "All men will hate you because of me" (Matthew 10:22). This is one promise that is not found in many promise boxes.

As we saw in the first part, many of the clues to Jesus' nature seem uniquely designed to reveal the intent and character of the Father and are not direct commands for us to fulfill. For instance, I cannot be born in a barn of questionable parents receiving a common name and angelic announcement. Though I grew up in poverty and in a bad neighborhood, that is of no redemptive significance to you. The same would be true of other marks of Jesus such as his motley crew and shameful death.

Though these are merely indicators of his nature for us and might not be copyable, his nature as expressed in the "greatest in the kingdom" teachings and in Philipians 2:5-11 are definitely within our reach.

Who is the greatest in the kingdom of heaven?

"Whoever wants to become great among you must be your servant, and whoever wants to be first must be slave of all."

"You know that those who are regarded as rulers of the Gentiles lord it over them, and their high officials exercise authority over them. Not so with you."

"Now that I, your Lord and Teacher, have washed your feet, you also should wash one another's feet. I have set you an example that you should do as I have done for you. I tell you the truth, no servant is greater than his master."

"Therefore, whoever humbles himself like this child is the greatest in the kingdom of heaven."

"Let the little children come to me, and do not hinder them, for the kingdom of God belongs to such as these."

"The greatest among you should be like the youngest, and the one who rules like the one who serves."

"If anyone wants to be first, he must be the very last."

"For he who is least among you all — he is the greatest."

Mark 10:43-44; 10:42-43; John 13:14-16;
Matthew 18:4; Mark 10:14; Luke 22:26;
Mark 9:35; Luke 9:48

At Your Service

Whoever wants to be first must be slave of all

When Jesus began to teach the disciples what it meant to be greatest in the kingdom, he was teaching about his own nature, for indeed he was, and is, the greatest in the kingdom. By that time, the disciples had had the opportunity to observe the servanthood of Christ, and they understood what he meant.

So the greatest must be slave of all, a servant. How totally opposed to all of my natural leanings. My culture teaches me that if I follow the clean-living precepts of Christianity, God will reward me with prosperity and with a consistent rise in status until I become boss, maybe even president. How strange that the true nature of Jesus would be so different from my ambitious view.

How would my family react if I were to come home and brag to them that I had been chosen as slave? Probably not with much glee! In fact, it isn't something I would want to boast about. Maybe nothing about the nature of Jesus and my living it out lends itself to advertising.

One way I try to get around servanthood is to select a "nice" clientele that I can serve gladly. But the Scriptures won't allow me to escape with such thinking. Jesus said, ". . . servant of all."

A servant's job is to do all he can to make life better for others — to free them to be everything they can be. A servant's first interest is not himself but others. Yet, enslavement is not what I am talking about. Servanthood is a loving choice we make to minister to others. It is not the result of coercion or coercion's more subtle form, manipulation.

Don't Trip on the Doormat

There is no joy in being a doormat even if it is a "Jesus doormat." We can easily fall prey to manipulation and become merely a doormat unless we understand the underlying dynamics of manipulation and how the nature of Jesus prevents it.

Manipulation permeates our relationships with each other. Through crafty and coercive means we get others to do our bidding. When they succumb to our cleverness, we do not respect them for it — indeed we often despise them. And when they don't give in, we often, with righteous indignation, instruct them on how they should be willing to serve us.

I have had people ask me to do what I knew was

not the best thing for them, and when I refused as graciously as I could, they would say, "But I thought you were a Christian. Aren't Christians supposed to do things like this?" That is a guilt-gotcha! When I don't want to do something but give in to keep from feeling guilty or losing face with significant persons or when I am afraid not to do it, then I have been manipulated.

When I have been manipulated, I feel even worse. I know I have been "had" again, and my self-esteem takes another drop. Perhaps the strongest form of manipulation used on me is when people hint that if a Christian ever did a certain something for them, they might consider becoming a Christian. Of course, the situation works its way around until it becomes a question of whether I will be the one who will bring them into the kingdom by so doing.

Sometimes we are forced to do things by people who withhold love or money from us until we do. Parents at times manipulate children by feigning sickness unless the child obeys. The list could go on.

Jesus had some classic cases in which people tried to manipulate him. Some of the Pharisees and Herodians were sent to catch him in his words:

> They came to him and said, "Teacher, we know you are a man of integrity. You aren't swayed by men, because you pay no attention to who they are; but you teach the way of God in accordance with the truth. Is it right to pay taxes to Caesar or not? Should we pay or shouldn't we?"

But Jesus knew their hypocrisy. "Why are you trying to trap me?" he asked. (Mark 12:13-15)

The chief means of resisting manipulation is humility — knowing who we really are and facing it. Jesus knew himself and was at ease with himself, so he was not swayed by their flattery. Had it been me, I would probably have thought that at last I was being recognized by these people for my true worth and now would be a good time to wax eloquent. There is nothing wrong in receiving true affirmation, but humility is sensitive to flattery and knows when it is occurring.

Jesus resisted manipulation vigorously, as he had done in a previous encounter:

The Pharisees came and began to question Jesus. To test him, they asked for a sign from heaven. He sighed deeply and said, "Why does this generation ask for a miraculous sign? I tell you the truth, no sign will be given to it." Then he left them, got back into the boat and crossed to the other side. (Mark 8:11-13)

Jesus knew the Pharisees were there for hostile reasons and not to get help. Often, such hostility is clear. Out of his humility (being who he was and not less or more), Jesus was able to express the anger he felt at the moment. Then because further interaction was not profitable, he withdrew from them.

A secondary method of resisting manipulation

then, is withdrawal. Jesus used it more than once. John records that "Jesus, knowing that they intended to come and make him king by force, withdrew again into the hills by himself" (John 6:15).

A particular characteristic of manipulation is that it destroys our ability to choose. It forces us to move defensively into the pattern or mold that others have chosen for us. Not a single person who tried to manipulate Jesus got the answer they expected. All of them received an expression of the true feelings of Jesus. From some of them he withdrew. In each case he protected his ability to choose.

There is a distinctive difference between coerced slavery and servanthood by choice. When Jesus stated that he chose to lay down his life and that no one was taking it from him, he was describing the basic element of love. Love always chooses to do the right and serving things for others — but it is a choice. You can only love by choice. True love cannot be the result of either decree, force or manipulation. Anything that I do to deprive someone of the right to choose is a violation of his personhood. When I sense that my own right to choose is being threatened, then I know that I am not being loved, and the doors are not open to ministry.

In humility, I can say something like this: "Although it may not be true, I am feeling pressured and manipulated. I am not able to choose and act out of love when I feel this way, so I am removing myself from the situation until I feel free to make the choice I feel is right."

Sometimes, when manipulation is detected in a

request, a simple no is the right thing to say. A demand for a reason is often part of the manipulative process. We must, in order to properly resist, know that we don't need to give the answer, but we do need to live with integrity so that we can have the power to make loving, others-oriented choices.

Often, when we say no, the person who has been trying to coerce us will create a scene. That, too, is part of the manipulative process. And it is included in the price to be paid if we wish to keep our integrity. But don't let the scene fool you. It can also be part of the healing process for the manipulator.

To be a manipulator is to be a sick person. If we permit someone to manipulate us, then we have contributed to and reinforced that person's sickness. To resist manipulation, though it may be difficult and may cause scenes, is to contribute to that person's health and certainly to contribute to our own health.

Another form of manipulation that often befalls persons trying to live the Jesus life is self-directed. We see the needs of the world and realize that the world needs us, yet there is so little of us. Then we are unable to rest. We try to respond to every genuine need that comes along until we have totally exhausted our resources and collapse into a bruised pile saying that we can never try to live the Jesus style again.

Once more, humility provides the answer for us. We are not God. So we can quit trying to be him and, in our finiteness, trying to solve all the world's problems. When we are honest about ourselves and recognize that we are running out of steam, then it is proper to be in seclusion and rest for a while. Jesus was often taking the disciples to places to rest. Though he was God, he refused the manipulation of his own life. He always kept his strength to make loving choices. And he calls us to make the loving choices necessary to be servant of all.

The Power Pyramid

Rulers of the Gentiles lord it over them . . .
Not so with you

It amazes me how many of our church and religious systems break apart when analyzed in terms of this command, and yet we continue claiming our structure to be biblical and authorized of God.

The principle of being servant to all is devastating to chains of command and to systems where submission is upward. Many religious structures are carbon copies of the flow-charts of giant corporations where the "lording" system is pyramid shaped. In the kingdom of God, the power pyramid is reversed, up-ended, so that the authority is on the bottom, not the top.

When Jesus alludes to submission, it is always directed toward leaders or the ones who want to be great in the kingdom and they are always ordered to submit downward, not upward. For example, in Matthew 20:17, Jesus expressly says, "whosoever will be chief among you, let him be your servant."

This downward submission of the greatest seems to be a natural outgrowth of the way Jesus viewed people. He served them because he knew their value. We lord it over others because we don't recognize their value and don't view them in the way Jesus does.

Those who lead in the kingdom of God are to recognize that every Christian has a unique and direct relationship to Christ, the head of the church. Unlike world systems whose goal is control, the kingdom leader is chosen to equip people for ministry, to bring unity in faith and knowledge, and to mature people so as to provide stability. (See Ephesians 4:11-16.)

Jesus reserved his strongest words for the spiritual leaders of his day. He was moved with compassion for the masses who were as sheep without a shepherd. He put no pressure on the masses to submit to the leader, but instead put the pressure on leaders to be slaves of all.

"I'm in Charge Here"

I am constantly hearing pronouncements from leaders of this day about how their followers, the masses, should be honest with them, how their followers should be obedient, how they should support, how they should submit. However, whether followers are free to respond honestly and without coercion in all these ways is entirely the responsibility of the leader.

First of all, just as Jesus did, leaders are to take the servant initiative to reveal their lives. Unfortunately, few preachers and other religious leaders are intimately known to those to whom they minister. Because of the training they have received or books they have read, many ministers feel they must maintain a professional distance from the people, thereby placing themselves above others. That stance has devastating and built-in problems. Someone who is at the top of a pyramid of authority finds himself isolated from reality. Those beneath him no longer give complete honesty. The "top" person is told by those under him only what is necessary to protect their jobs. The only means by which the person at the top can be assured of honesty and truthfulness from those beneath him is to make himself of "no reputation" — to lay aside his power and authority and approach them as a servant. And that initiative must first be taken by the person at the top. It cannot come from those beneath him — only revolution comes from that direction. In the nature of Jesus, it is only possible to submit downward in the human realm.

I read in an article once about a person who had completely submitted himself to a leader. The leader, in order to teach the submitted person servanthood, required that person to mow the leader's lawn. That is a perversion of the Jesus style. Servanthood should be taught by mowing the other person's lawn.

One who leads in the style of Jesus does not use forms of coercion nor does he depend on institutional position for authority. Instead, by serving people, he leads as they recognize his ability and choose voluntarily to follow. And those who follow, by whatever means, will become like their leader for better or worse.

A religious leader, under fire once for using his position for personal gain, defended himself by stating to his followers that he hadn't done anything that they would not have done had they had the chance. In other words, if they could have gotten away with it, they would have, also. That statement was the greatest indictment against their system and ethical training that could have been made.

Perhaps a good way to handle the trappings of leadership would be to put *Slave* over the doors of our plush offices and take away everything from the surroundings that is incompatible with that. Remember, power corrupts and absolute power corrupts absolutely.

A slave should have no title that raises him above that lowly level and definitely no title that raises him above others. A slave should have no status symbols except the scars that come from hard work. You would not expect a slave to have a special parking space more accessible than his master's. A slave would not have an office larger than others or more ornately decorated in order to show his position. A slave would not wear clothing that intimidated others or impressed them in any way except as being their servant. A slave would not use his position to limit the expression of his master's capabilities. A slave would not try to use his "power" to protect his position of "first."

There are so many ways that the nature of Jesus is in direct opposition to the leadership patterns of the world that have been unquestioningly adopted by the church that this list could go on and on. This is indeed unfortunate, for it is that visible modeling that has greater force than the expression of doctrine. We have been so careful to identify doctrinal heresy; perhaps it is time to identify heresy of practice.

"But people are dumb sheep and need to be motivated," I have often heard in defense of the world's system. If we wish to admit that we are not the church and intend to have no part of Jesus, then we can motivate people any way we wish to get them to do our bidding. But if we wish to be followers of Jesus, then we must be lovers of people, and any motivation must come out of their voluntary response to love — even if it doesn't seem as rapid or as efficient as the experts tell us it can be. We cannot finish with worldly systems what was begun by Jesus working through the Holy Spirit.

What would happen to the body of Christ if we all treated each other in keeping with the nature of Jesus and our leaders lived it out for us first? My mind is staggered at the possibility. What we do now has been taught to us, so we certainly could be taught something different. Were it so, the world would beat our doors down to be a part of the church.

Both Sides of the Coin

Perhaps the most significant place to begin to turn the power pyramid upside down is in the family. The world's first institution has had some rough going. Some of the chuck holes in the road of marriage have been placed there by the teachings of various religious systems. To see how the nature of Jesus dramatically affects marriage, let us look first at some of the current teaching.

"At the top of every chain of command is a man." All women are somewhere down the scale. Access to God is often prohibited unless through the authorization of a man. Current teaching especially emphasizes this in the marriage bond. The mainstay of such teaching is in Ephesians where Paul says wives should submit to their husbands as unto the Lord.

Books by women for women also take advantage of this understanding of submission and support it with an interesting twist. Women can be taught how to get their man to do what they want him to do by using the strength of sex and this clever thing called submission. It is degrading, but at least the women win eventually. Consequently, men are forced into the role of being God, which they can't handle, and women are forced into the role of weak underling, which they don't want. Submission gone sour is the result of not understanding the nature of Jesus.

Let us look at the Ephesians passage thoroughly, but let's start a little earlier than some others do:

Submit to one another out of reverence for Christ. Wives, submit to your husband as to the Lord. For the husband is the head of the wife as Christ is the head of the church, his body, of which he is the Savior. Now as the church submits to Christ, so also wives should submit to their husbands in everything.

Husbands, love your wives, just as Christ loved the church and gave himself up for her . . . . (Ephesians 5:21-25)

So, the first command is to submit ourselves to each other. That is the way a body would work. Then the next commands are enlargements on the first. They tell us how submission works its way out in a marriage relationship: Wives to the husband as unto the Lord; husbands loving the wives as Christ loved the church.

The wife's position has been rather clear for a long time. But what is the description of the husband to whom she submits? Well, how did Christ love the church? He came to the church as a slave, not lording it over them, being an example, being humble, being as a child, being as the least, as the younger, as the last, using no force, being of no reputation, obedient to this nature even to death. Any time I treat my wife in this manner, submission is never a point of contention. And submission that is coerced is not submission. Remember, too, that the burden of initiating the slave role rests on the leader or head.

Humility then permits husband and wife to work out differences without violating one another. Rather than attacking and accusing when arguments occur, they can be honest about their own feelings.

It is important to note that in God's new order we

are all members of the family of God before we are members of our earthly family. So my wife is my sister in Christ before she is my wife. Thus, I must treat her as God's child and with even greater care than I would expect someone to treat my own children. I dare not be superior and manipulative with one of God's children.

Seen and Not Hurt

How can we be a servant to our children and not spoil them? Actually, servanthood is the best guarantee of their spiritual health. If we understand that our children are God's children first, then we understand that we are rearing them in his behalf as his servant and theirs. Consequently, we will be willing to train and discipline them out of our servanthood in order to reproduce the Spirit of their Father in them.

Servanthood causes us to be present with our children, in touch with and meeting their needs, alert to their tendencies to wander from the nature of the Father and committed to confront that wandering. Servanthood means making right choices in behalf of children and sticking to them. Servanthood means saying no when no is for their benefit. It is also consistent with Paul's admonition: "Fathers, do not exasperate your children; instead, bring them up in the training and instruction of the Lord" (Ephesians 6:4). Living the Jesus style will not exasperate children but will cause them to know they are loved.

Servanthood means equipping children for independent adulthood and then turning them back to their other Father. It means neither strictness nor permissiveness: it means appropriateness.

To be placed by God as the slave in charge of his children is an awesome responsibility. But no matter what the circumstances, God honors the servant-love of parents.

When I was six years old, my father was severely injured in an airplane accident and was left partially paralyzed and brain damaged. My mother then became the breadwinner of the house.

Since my mother was often "not there" as she attempted to make a living and my dad "not there" physically or mentally, the stage was set for family failure. But our family did not fail! Through difficult times, both parents stayed faithful to God and to us. Prayer, belief, steadfastness and love surrounded us — money and fine homes didn't.

When my father died, my two brothers and I stood in front of his casket and made the following statement to the friends who had gathered for the funeral service: "Our father did not leave a financial empire for us to carry on. Many things that a dad normally does with his sons, ours was unable to do. He was unable to teach us many things that a dad normally teaches. But he did leave us something that he had. He left us with a love of God, a love for the Bible, a love of people, an understanding of worship and an inability to hate. We feel that he has left us only those things that will last. So we stand before you as his sons and declare publicly that we will follow his God."

Servant-parents who value deeply the gift of God in their home recognize the privilege and responsibility to carefully tend God's garden of life. Thus their children are reared with fewer bruises, stronger spirits and healthier personalities. The fact that Jesus was reared in a bad neighborhood is evidence that servanthood does not require ideal family or physical situations for success. Nor does it require financial opulence. It requires only our obedience to the servant nature of Jesus.

I'd Rather See a Sermon

*I have set you an example that you should do
as I have done for you*

My wife and family were once braving a 400 mile journey to join me at a camp where I was speaking. Their trip took them at first through a large city whose street configuration was rather confusing. For two hours they tried to make it through the city. They sought directions from policemen and others who would know. But each attempt to follow the directions was met with frustration.

Finally, on the edge of despair, they stopped at another service station for one more attempt to get adequate instructions. With each direction given, my family responded, "But we tried that. It didn't work." Then a man who overheard the conversation said, "I am in this red car parked here. You follow me. I will show you the way."

So through the jungle of streets he led them, guiding them through difficult intersections until they were several miles beyond the city. When only the main highway remained, he stopped and said, "Now you can't get lost. Just keep going on this road." That man was like Jesus to my family. I don't know if he was a follower of Jesus, but he certainly had a better understanding of the leadership style of Jesus than many of us who are his followers do.

The most effective form of Christian leadership is leadership by example. Jesus didn't say, "Do as I say, not as I do." Rather, as Matthew reports:

> Jesus said to the crowds and to the disciples: "The teachers of the law and the Pharisees sit in Moses' seat. So you must obey them and do everything they tell you. But do not do what they do, for they do not practice what they preach. They tie up heavy loads and put them on men's shoulders, but they themselves are not willing to lift a finger to move them.
>
> "Everything they do is done for men to see: They make their phylacteries wide and the tassels of their prayer shawls long; they love the place of honor at banquets and the most important seats in the synagogues; they love to be greeted in the marketplaces and to have men call them 'Rabbi.'
>
> "But you are not to be called 'Rabbi,' for you have only one Master and you are all brothers. And do not call anyone on earth 'father,' for you have one Father, and he is in heaven. Nor are you to be called 'teacher,' for you have one Teacher, the Christ. The

greatest among you will be your servant."
(Matthew 23:1-11)

In God's army, generals are not in protected posts behind the lines. No, their position is at the front of the troops, exposing themselves first to the best fire the enemy has to offer and showing how the battle is won.

I listened in disbelief once as a theology student complained that the college he was in didn't have a separate dormitory for "his kind" so they wouldn't be disturbed and corrupted by those not interested in the "ministry."

This age has joined with the age of Jesus in removing the influence of believers from sinners. Everywhere, Christian ghettos are springing up. The light is hidden under church pews rather than shining openly. We stand away from the sinner as he sweeps helplessly to his doom and safely advise him not to sweep helplessly to his doom!

But Jesus was Emmanuel — God *with* us, and he bids us follow him. He didn't "lord it over" the disciples. He never asked them to do anything that he had not done first and shown them how to do. If we really love people as Jesus did, we will involve ourselves with them in showing them how.

Teaching Without Walls

While teaching at a Christian college, I noticed that my lecturing on prayer and asking good questions about prayer on tests did not teach the students how to pray. All that system taught them was how to take notes and how to answer test questions. I was able to teach prayer only to those with whom I prayed.

A leading professor in a well-known seminary candidly admitted that his seminary did not train people to pastor; it trained people to teach in seminary, because that is the example set for them in the classroom. Jesus chose modeling rather than the classroom as his intimate style of teaching. To learn an attitude or skill that we have not seen performed is extremely difficult. I am thankful that a driver taught me to drive an automobile; that gentle hands guided mine to tie my own shoelaces.

If the old cliche — those who can, do; those who can't, teach — were true, there would be no teaching because teaching is guided doing. Also, it is in modeling that one can be truly last by going first. When students are experiencing anxiety at the prospect of going first in some new activity, the teacher, by taking the unfavored role of being first, performs an act of servanthood much like that of the king's food taster in history.

Education is what we call the process of passing along knowledge and values and the process of shaping behavior. For the Christian there is a dimension beyond that — the passing along of life. Only life begets life.

For years the church has taken its signals on how to educate from the world and not from Jesus who said, "A student is not above his teacher, but everyone who is fully trained will be like his teacher" (Luke 6:40). We have brought students away from life into a classroom. Jesus drew students into the middle of life. We have limited the time for education to an hour or two. Jesus gave all his time to educating his disciples. We have gloried in ever-larger classes. Jesus chose twelve to be "with him." We have kept teachers in isolated non-revealing lecture roles. Jesus exposed his life to the disciples. We dump our children into a reservoir of bodies and leave their training to strangers. The Bible gives the first responsibility to parents.

If you are a teacher struggling with a classroom setting or some other limitation imposed upon you, the following principles should be seen as an encouraging call rather than a frustrating lack.

Education in the Jesus style has teachers who walk with students, revealing their own lives and struggles — teachers who fulfill the servant qualities of Jesus. Education in the Jesus style recognizes that the student is the reason for being, not the teacher or administrator, and shapes its actions accordingly.

Education in the Jesus style trains people to be members of the kingdom first, not citizens of the United States or any country first. The teachers and other workers, in their chosen structure, model the kingdom for the students.

Education in the Jesus style prepares the home to be the major force for spiritual training. Education in the Jesus style discerns the difference between the law of love in the kingdom of God and the forces of culture and tradition and does not teach culture and tradition as the kingdom way.

Education in the Jesus style keeps the number of students for any teacher limited to the number he or she can love and closely associate with. Education in the Jesus style does not use any means of evaluation that will lessen a person's view of himself.

Education in the Jesus style does not build any system of discipline that is not born out of and supported by an intimate relationship with the disciplinarians.

Education in the Jesus style uses as its criterion the equipping of the students to be everything God has gifted them to be. It does not use a profile of other expectations as a mold into which they must fit.

Education in the Jesus style views the long-term impact and prepares for the whole of life. It is not subservient to fads or programs to benefit the educational system rather than the student.

Education in the Jesus style recognizes love as the goal of life and not knowledge for its own sake. It recognizes that knowledge of God properly taught produces lives that love as Jesus loved, live as he lived.

No More, No Less

*Whoever humbles himself like this child is the
greatest in the kingdom of heaven*

I had long misunderstood humility. Thinking
it to be like an inferiority complex, I adopted
a properly despondent look and asserted that I
was nothing — I couldn't sing, couldn't preach,
couldn't play the piano or any other instrument,
was barely coordinated enough to walk. People
would respond as expected by saying, "My, you are
so humble." In all "humility" I would thank them
for noticing.

Now, I realize that this attitude was not humility, it
was sickness. Humility is no hangdog approach to
life. Humility is simply seeing ourselves as we actually are, not higher nor lower. It means being gut-
level honest about ourselves — being up front. It
means knowing who we are and owning that — and
owning our emotions. It means living without
hypocrisy.

In the desert, Moses had an encounter with God through the burning bush. After agreeing to return to Egypt to lead the children of Israel out, Moses wanted to be sure no one was playing a practical joke on him, so he asked for the voice to identify itself. What company name was going to be on the business card? God replied, "I am who I am." God is congruent. He is who he is. Jesus also said, "I am the way, the truth and the life" and, "Before Abraham was, I am." Humility is being an "I am."

One of the most loving things I can do for someone is to be honest (humble) about myself so they don't have to sift through my deceptions. I doubt that when Jesus greeted the disciples in the mornings they had to ponder over what he really meant. His being the same "yesterday, today and forever," probably didn't mean that he had no emotions or moods, but may have meant that he was always honest about them; always an "I am."

Jesus was willing for people to see him intimately:

They said, "Rabbi" (which means, Teacher), "where are you staying?"
"Come," he replied, "and you will see." (John 1:38-39)

Especially note that Jesus' openness did not come as a result of probes or congressional investigations. His openness came at his own initiative. He did not have the philosophy that "what they don't know won't hurt them."

Jesus chose the disciples to be "with him," a state

of relationship that can only be revealing. In "with-ness" we see behind the social graces to the realities of everyday life. When my wife and I were courting, we carefully dressed, combed and deodorized our-selves. Not until the withness that marriage brings did she discover all of the uncouth actions of my physical being and begin to discover the nature of my motivations. Time and withness produces revelation.

Jesus was faithful in his revelation to the disciples. In his "graduation sermon" he states to them, "I have called you friends, for everything that I learned from my Father I have made known to you" (John 15:15). Friendship requires revelation.

Although the larger crowds benefited from the teaching of Jesus about openness and revelation, full intimacy was reserved for the disciples. Teaching about the Father was the most important thing for Jesus and that is what he did in the larger settings. Showing the Father was best done in more intimate relationships that would not be "casting pearls before swine." Jesus judiciously did not satisfy the curiosity seekers, but those who truly desired access to him attained it.

In our society (church and secular), the higher you go up the ladder, the more inaccessible you are to people — the more hidden your personal life is. The further Jesus went into his messianic ministry, the more his friends could see into the depths of his inner life and emotions.

In Broad Daylight

We are so unaccustomed to living openly that these are probably some of the most threatening words in Scripture:

> "Be on your guard against the yeast of the Pharisees, which is hypocrisy. There is nothing concealed that will not be disclosed or hidden that will not be made known. What you have said in the dark will be heard in the daylight, and what you have whispered in the ear in the inner rooms will be proclaimed from the housetops." (Luke 12:1-3)

Humility might well be described as "walking in the light." Humility chooses to be real, to hide nothing, to be open. This certainly is a loving way to be toward people. The progression in 1 John 1:7, then, is logical: "But if we walk in the light, as he is in the light, we have fellowship with one another, and the blood of Jesus, his Son, purifies us from every sin."

Our attitudes and values are so rarely derived from living scriptural principles that we are utterly out of touch with the power that comes from living in the light. We fear the vulnerability of it. Knowing the changes we will have to go through causes us great anxiety.

Yet, we need not fear that people will see our imperfections. We join the human race in having them. Our rejoicing is in the fact that we are forgiven and are growing.

All of us are sinners and I am not sure that some sinners are really greater sinners than others. It is just that some sins are more visible than others. I can cover up well on the outside and still "regard iniquity in my heart." Jesus indicated that those who are forgiven much, love much. This could mean that those who are fully repentant of both inner and outer sins are now fully visible and open. They feel the complete redemption of God, thereby enabling them to spend their energies loving much. But the Pharisees, whose outsides were whitewashed, had not repented of the inner hidden sins and were thus handicapped in their ability to love.

The Cost of Hiding

Any secret, whether good or bad, produces, according to psychologists, the same guilt effects on our being that sin does. Any strong emotion, positive ones included, that we contain and store up, rather than learning how to express, works on our being and our environment in unhealthy ways.

Our true nature is not designed for us to hide ourselves. The efforts toward covering that began at the fall of mankind are typical of the whole earthly lifestyle. The energy that goes into hiding is costly to us as persons. Anything we hide forces us to live in a way that will keep what we hide safely hidden. In other words, we become unreal — untrue to ourselves — incongruent. That unreality is opposite to the nature of Jesus who is the God of reality. No energy was spent in covering his life with a mask. In him, there was no darkness at all.

The poignant statement, "Jesus wept," recorded by John is evidence that even publicly Jesus was free to be real with all of his inner being. His angers were openly expressed. The compassions that moved him, his joys, his griefs were obvious enough that the writers of the Gospels could observe and record them.

Only through humility are we able to properly handle strong emotions. The Bible tells us to be angry and sin not and not to let the sun set on our anger. We tend to interpret that as meaning we are to keep a stiff upper lip. Don't reveal your anger. Grit your teeth. Grin and bear it.

The opposite response that occasionally breaks out when we have gritted our teeth as long as we can is to use violence or even subtle vengeance. Neither violence nor sublimation are healthy ways of handling anger. Humility permits me to own my feelings — to admit them. Now, I am free to say, "I am angry." I am free to admit what I am reacting to. I am free to ask if anger is what the person wanted to produce in me and to ask for help in changing if my reaction is inappropriate.

This ability to express our true feelings out of humility extends even to our relationship with God. When events in nature occur that frustrate and anger us, we subtly label them as "acts of God" to show our feelings. Would expressing anger outright to God be any more dangerous? Do you suppose God is affected by diplomacy or flattery?

Since most of our prayers are basically complaints about how God is running the world, would honesty about feelings we have toward God or disappointments we experience in our relationship with him be out of order? The beauty of intimate relationships is that they not only survive emotional expressions but are often enriched by them. Is the *abba* relationship with God too fragile for that or do we fear fierce retaliation from the author of mercy? Even Jesus cried in that despairing moment, "Why hast thou forsaken me?"

It is striking how we, because of cultural influences, are trained to hide our feelings. Sadly, some Christian groups are taught that we must smile through the deepest of hurts. They even deny that these hurts exist, thinking that Christians must always and only be positive, joyful and smiling. How often couples who are going through difficulties journey to church unsmiling, not speaking, until just outside the door when they put on "the smile." When the official greeter asks how they are doing, the standard smiling response comes, "Just fine, thank you."

If there is one place where we ought to be able to come with our sins and feelings exposed and find help and healing, it is the church. But more and more it has become the one place where we must be the most careful to hide our true feelings and instead support the appearance of consistent gleeful victory.

The body of Christ, especially in well-functioning, small, intimate groups, is the most healing body in the world; yet we do not treat it as such. We wouldn't think of relating to a medical doctor with the same reserve as we have in the healing body of Christ. Would we say to a doctor, "I have this unspoken illness"? Of course not! But we often use the term *unspoken request* in sharing our needs with the body. Would we try to deceive a doctor into thinking our hurt is nonexistent or in a different place than it actually is? Of course not! Would we say, "I am here for a friend — examine me and diagnose him"? Of course not! Yet we will treat the church with such distrust and fear. We choose to hide. Somehow we have decided that the church is supposed to be the company of the perfect rather than the company of the forgiven. This attempt to keep up appearances has brought the church to a crisis of honesty in which reality has fallen by the wayside as we attempt to project for all to see a facsimile of the ideal. Meanwhile, we desperately hope that the truth is not discovered — that the facade is accepted. In the name of Christ, we cover our own sins and failings and crucify those in our ranks who would dare cry foul and bring our "mistakes" out into the light.

Sir Walter Scott spoke of the nature of humility when he said: "Oh, what a tangled web we weave, when first we fashion to deceive." When by my incongruency I give people wrong signals, they respond accordingly and wrongly. Then I respond wrongly to their wrong response. On and on this cycle continues until a war is started and no one remembers how it began.

Paul underscored the importance of openness in the church when he wrote to the Philippians, "Whatever you have . . . seen in me — put it into practice" (Philippians 4:9). To the Thessalonians he wrote, "We have loved you so much that we were delighted to share with you not only the gospel of God but our lives as well, because you had become so dear to us" (1 Thessalonians 2:8).

In writing to the Corinthians he developed the concept further:

> We are not like Moses, who would put a veil over his face to keep the Israelites from gazing at it while the radiance was fading away . . . Now the Lord is the Spirit, and where the Spirit of the Lord is, there is freedom. And we, who with unveiled faces all reflect the Lord's glory, are being transformed into his likeness with ever-increasing glory, which comes from the Lord, who is the Spirit. (2 Corinthians 3:13,17,18)

I had always used these verses declaring freedom where the Spirit is to justify some of the more bizarre aspects of enthusiastic church life. Now, I see that the presence of the Holy Spirit frees me to rip off my veil (mask) and walk openly, not because I am perfect, but because I am now reflecting the Lord's glory and am being transformed — constantly improving, growing.

Moses veiled his face to hide his weakness. He chose to do so. Apparently there was no real need to do that; however, whenever we operate under the law, human frailty (perhaps especially in the face of great spiritual experiences) forces us to pretend, to hide, to cover up in order to put our best foot forward for all to see.

Grace is so different in its fulfillment of the law. John tells us (1:17) that the law came by Moses; grace and truth by Jesus Christ. The law demanded righteousness — grace delivered righteousness. The law required — grace provided. The law was pressure — grace was relief. The law was bondage — grace was freedom. Grace and truth can only be modeled in the light, in being seen. Because of the very nature of grace, we have no reason to hide: "Whoever lives by the truth comes into the light, so that it may be seen plainly that what he has done has been done through God" (John 3:21).

To live with a mask is not to experience the freedom of the Spirit who administers forgiveness and gives us courage to rip the veil aside and reflect God's glory. We are free to do so, not because we have reached a stage of perfection that would guard us from the embarrassing gaze of the world, but because, unlike Moses, we are not "fading away" but are instead increasing or growing in God's likeness.

In the plan of God, everything said, done or thought will be revealed. For those who hide, it will be disaster. For the open and growing, it will merely be redeemed history.

A Child Is. . .

Let the little children come to me . . . for the kingdom of God belongs to such as these

Jesus had a special place in his heart for children, and through them he taught the disciples a needed lesson.

People were bringing little children to Jesus to have him touch them, but the disciples rebuked them. When Jesus saw this, he was indignant. He said to them, "Let the little children come to me, and do not hinder them, for the kingdom of God belongs to such as these. I tell you the truth, anyone who will not receive the kingdom of God like a little child will never enter it." And he took the children in his arms, put his hands on them and blessed them. (Mark 10:13-16)

A child is unthreatening. I would not mind meeting a child in a dark alley. If we are to follow the footsteps of Jesus and represent him correctly, the world must be no more threatened by us than we would be by a child. Jesus even states: "I am sending you out like sheep among wolves. Therefore be as shrewd as snakes and as innocent as doves" (Matthew 10:16).

Some years ago, when I was an associate pastor in Illinois, the ladies of the church would come on Thursday mornings for a prayer meeting. Since it was a ladies' meeting and I was not invited, I chose to go and spend time in the nursery playing with their children. I shall never forget the first time I did it. Opening the top half of the nursery door, I leaned in and said, "Hi, kids. Pastor Erwin here. Let's play!" One of them ran into another room, frightened. The others merely went about their business. Well, they didn't seem to understand who I was, I thought, so I entered the room, walked to the middle of the group and said again, "Hi, kids. Let's play!" Another one ran into the adjoining room, terrified. The remainder continued their actions as if to say, "Did you hear a noise?"

By this point my ego was getting involved. The nursery attendant had begun to smile in amusement. I wanted to grab one of them and shake him and say, "You are going to play with me and you are going to enjoy it. Do you hear me?" But then, the Holy Spirit helped me to remember what adults looked like when I was that size. They were frightening giants. My world was kneecap height. I never carried on conversations with adults. What could we talk about? I knew nothing about politics. Economics was out. I thought a nickel was better than a dime because it was bigger. I was to be seen and not heard.

So, with this memory moving me, I fell to the floor and then said, "Hi, kids. Let's play!" In thirty seconds every one of them was on top of me squealing, pulling my tie, my hair — destroying my dignity. From then on, I played no role games. I would enter, hit the floor, and be considered a close friend — unthreatening.

The unthreatening childlikeness of Jesus intimidated no one. Both friend and foe approached him freely. The Pharisees and Saduccees attacked him with a fervor they could never have mustered had Jesus walked the earth with a heavenly glow and spoken in a royal, electronically enhanced voice. Children were comfortable around him, which even a surface observation would tell you could not be so without his own childlikeness. The Sanhedrin plotted to capture him and were held off, not by their fear of Jesus, but by their fear of the crowds.

A child isn't good at deceiving. Part of being like a child is to be humble, to be real. You can tell when children are happy or when they are sad. If they are afraid, they act accordingly. It is well known that any two children playing together will go through alternate stages of laughing, squealing, running, being angry and crying. When we affirm their freedom to do so, they can be terminally angry at a friend and five minutes later be playing again as if nothing had ever happened.

When my son was about five years old, he wanted

to take a toy out of his room that, because of its delicacy, we had instructed him to keep inside. He made the attempt, nonetheless. With arm behind him, bent over body, and furtive glance, he shuffled stealthily sideways in plain view of the whole family. What he was doing was written all over him. He didn't know how to sneak! But just give me a little time and I will teach him the sophisticated adult art of sneaking.

At one time he was interested in magic tricks, but their proper execution eluded him. You always knew where the hidden item was. It was in the "closed" hand. He didn't know how to deceive.

Most of us can picture those times we needed to give our children a spoonful of medicine. Their tightly clenched mouths formed the immovable object oblivious to our pleas to open up. Then with parental deception, we would say, "Look, it *is* good. See? I will take some first and show you." Then we would sip a little of the foul-tasting brew but smile as if we had embarked on a gourmet feast. The now-convinced child opens his mouth and learns quickly that to be grown up means to lie and deceive.

If I thought someone I loved was cheating on me or in some way trying to deceive me, how would it affect me? How would it change my relationship with others if I knew they wouldn't deceive me? Deception is not compatible with childlikeness, love or Jesus.

I enjoy telling stories to children. They can suspend their disbelief so easily. If I tell them something as the truth they accept it as such. They are adept at accepting things at face value. Apparently, this is precisely the way Jesus requires us to accept the kingdom of God. It is first and primarily a matter of our belief — we chose to accept — before it ever becomes part of our logic.

A child is innocent. When Jesus told us we must be as a little child in receiving the kingdom, he was using as an example one who had not yet come under the requirements of the law. Only after a certain age was a child considered accountable and under the command of the law. Until then, he was innocent. To receive the grace and forgiveness of God as a child would is to understand that we are now in a state of innocence. How difficult it is for me to accept the forgiveness of God that way. I continue to lay different types of laws and requirements on myself and others. I find it so difficult to accept my state as being "just as if I had never sinned." I keep trying to earn the acceptance and forgiveness of God. Until I accept this forgiveness and innocence, I will minister to others out of guilt and my own needs rather than being free to be totally oriented toward them, sensitive to them, serving them.

The Hand-Me-Down Set

The greatest among you should be like the youngest

Firstborns always did have it better. Statistically they achieve more, reach higher positions, score higher on IQ tests, etc. They receive more undivided attention from their parents than subsequent children. They are given responsibility earlier and that provides for more rapid maturity. In a real sense, the elder needs little outside help. He has it made.

Not so, the younger. First of all, he has to deal with the problem of a somewhat arrogant elder brother. That can give him lifelong hangups. Many of his possessions are second-hand offerings from the brother who has outgrown them or used them. The standard by which he is judged is often the elder brother. His identity is tied up with him in the school system — "Oh yes, you are so-and-so's brother." He is expected to excel in the same areas his brother did. Much of life becomes an odyssey to discover just who he himself is.

Being the younger is, by its nature, not a position of strength or authority. It does not speak dominance. It tends to be a position that waits and accepts whatever comes to it after others have had first choice.

When Jesus used the word *younger* it was filled with much more meaning than it has today. The younger brother was stereotypically a rebel — a person who had no stake in the status quo. The system under which he lived was an oppressor to him. Success in life depended upon his own abilities and the mercy of others. Life in general and tradition in particular were not a benefactor to him. The elder received the birthright and in some cases all of the inherited property. Why shouldn't the youngest be a rebel? Power was strictly on the other side. Even the slightest self-preservative action would brand him as a rebel by the "elders" in control.

In contrast, the elder brothers had a vested interest in the existing system. Just by birth order they had secured future positions. For them, the watchword was "Protect the status quo." ("Things are working well now. Let's keep them that way.") Elders were the governors. The positions of authority went to them. As far as this world is concerned, it was the most advantageous position to be in.

But Jesus said we must be as the younger — even if we are elders. Any power or advantage we have that is not handled as if we were the younger is a violation of the nature of Jesus. For the status quo power systems of the world and the church, this is a declaration of war.

Bringing Up the Rear

If anyone wants to be first, he must be the very last

The very last — how much this is in keeping with the whole lifestyle of one who would be a servant. But how different from our human nature.

When my family was young, we would travel together during the summers in a Volkswagen van and tent camp along the way to speaking engagements. It combined business and pleasure very well. After a drive of 200 miles or so, we would begin to be bone weary and I would pick a place to stop and rest — occasionally a small neighborhood park. Can you picture my children bounding out of the van, racing toward the only swing in the park and shouting all the way, "I'm last, I'm last, I'm last?" Don't try too hard to envision it, because it didn't and simply doesn't happen. The nature of our humanity drives us to be first.

This is a competitive age, but competition is meaningless unless there is a best or first to be gained and a competitor to be conquered. It is very difficult to compete with someone who chooses to be last, who refuses to join in the race to prove himself superior.

Whether I wish it to be so or not, being first means to relegate others to lesser positions. My superiority is always at the expense of someone else. So I have a choice — will I be self-seeking or will I love and serve others? So powerful is my selfishness that I will go to great lengths to prove that the Scripture permits me to be this way, that God just "wills" some of us to grab the brass ring — and who am I to argue with God? (I often find myself first in the art of rationalization.)

Sibling Rivalry

Because they seem good in our secular society, a host of customs have been brought across without question into the church. Competition is one of them. Early in our lives we are steeped in the concept of winning, getting there first, getting the most, garnering top honors. School is a daily dose of the competitive spirit. It provides a lot of enjoyment in what would otherwise be unbearably long times. It is unquestionably a good form of motivation. We work harder in a good competitive situation. But what are the implications of competition in the body of Christ?

No body can survive with its parts competing against each other. A body is designed to be healthy when each part is doing its job in a thoroughly cooperative manner. Competition, by its very nature, is self-serving — the very opposite of the servant, self-giving nature of Jesus. Some specific attributes of competition should prove our case.

For competition to work, there must be a prize — either a material one of value or else the prize of simply proving mastery over others and being number one.

First, to seek a material prize as the result of doing the work of God is to misunderstand or disobey Scripture: "For the kingdom of God is not a matter of eating and drinking, but of righteousness, peace and joy in the Holy Spirit . . ." (Romans 14:17).

Second, to desire to be master over others is to disobey the injunction to be last for the benefit of others. To seek and achieve a position over others is to feed one's pride. Without pride, the achievement of being better than others would be meaningless.

Because of the value of the prize and our drive toward it, competition tends to give rise to cheating. Rather than fostering the best attributes it brings out the things that go along with the spirit of materialism and pride.

I have discovered that I am a poor winner. When I have bettered someone, I gloat. I can't help it. It is the natural me. Sometimes, in "friendly" kidding, I will remind him frequently of the fact that I have beaten him. I can become rather obnoxious.

But if I am a poor winner, I am an even poorer loser. After losing, I ransack my storehouse of rationalizations. My feelings of jealousy and resentment toward anyone who would be so arrogant as to defeat me run rampant. From the moment of the loss I enter the scheming phase — planning for that moment when I can even the score. It dawned on me one day that the attitudes I had in both winning and losing had little Christlikeness about them.

Another problem of competition is that it can only measure the least significant of our actions. One can never give a prize for spirituality or faith or love because these cannot be measured. Instead we measure specific physical actions like the number of visitors brought to Sunday school or the most money collected for missions. The prize given for such actions gives a good clue to the actual motivation.

Every contest has to have rules. Who decides the rules? Someone sits down and comes up with a set of rules depending on what action the rule setter desires. This is a rather arbitrary way to let our lives be guided.

Perhaps the biggest problem for the health of the body of Christ is that competition creates so many losers and so few winners. To belong to Christ is to be a winner as far as eternity is concerned. Any activity that does not enhance that reality but instead rein-forces the common human feeling of being a loser does not fit within the pattern of the nature of Jesus.

People have argued vehemently with me that competition is fine within the body, that its fun and motivation make it worthwhile. The one thing that I have noticed is that only people who are accustomed to winning — those who by reason of their birth, not their choice, were blessed with strong and coordinated bodies and minds — are so vehement in defending competition. That seems to prove the whole point to me.

I do believe that competition can be redeemed. Making the prize valueless or only of value inherent within the action would be the first step (such as the sheer joy of the activity or of being with friends). Designing games so that athletic prowess is of no value and everyone, regardless of ability, is on equal footing would be a second step. Creating situations that build the spirit of fellowship more than the spirit of competition would be a third step. To devise means of giving the "less honorable parts . . . special honor" as Paul indicates in 1 Corinthians 12:22-25 would be a fourth step.

A subtle problem can arise that we must be aware of and resist. We are not to say, "Since I am the greatest, you be the first. I will be last." How nauseating! No, if we love others the way Jesus does, we will rejoice so much in seeing them achieve and enjoy the position of being first that we will hardly notice that in our efforts to help them, we turned up last. This is the result of the totally others-oriented servant.

The exciting question to be pondered is, "What would happen to the church if we all treated each other this way?" I believe this loving servanthood within the body of Christ would inspire the members and so captivate the hearts of searchers that the masses would seek us out. Love is irresistible. I long for the world's commentary to once again be, "My how those Christians love one another!"

It was out of the disciples' spirit of competition —

the desire to be greater than the other — that Jesus began to teach the opposite — the traits of the greatest in the Kingdom. If I am to live after the pattern of Jesus, it must touch every part of my life including that innate pride that drives me to defeat my brothers.

Room in the Manger

For he who is least among you all — he is the greatest

No prizes that I know of go to those who are least. Those who are least are not there for the glory it offers. Willingness to be the least is possible only if we are comfortable with ourselves and who we are. If it is injurious to us to lose face, then we will never choose to be least. If we have an unhealthy need for recognition and crave praise for accomplishment, then we won't go in the direction of the least.

Leaders with a desperate need for success have found awards and honors a profitable way to manipulate their followers. Dignified statesmen of the church have been shamelessly compromised for the sake of potential recognition.

Just as competition works only because of the drive for self-exaltation, so the fires of our desire for honor are fueled by a trait different from the one that motivated Jesus. He "made himself of no reputation."

Our violations of his nature in the area of honors and recognition are so obvious that I choose only to call a few to our attention.

The society I live in is an advertising and public relations oriented society. The weekly church page in the local newspaper is filled with the same self-chosen superlatives that Hollywood uses to present its product. What a judgment that it should be the least read page in the newspaper! Individual and corporate church public relations releases list accomplishments and honors in the same fashion that the world does. To hear the introductions given at Christian festivals and conventions is a painful experience in aggrandizement. The use of honorary degrees by Christian colleges to gain donations or other reciprocal benefits is a scandal. Some college honor plans are devised to cash in on vanity and sell books to the honored recipient. Some denominational public relations agents have as one of their job tasks to gain public honors for denominational hierarchy. I, to my shame, have worked intimately with others on honor-giving schemes designed to tap this weakness of humanity and move them to achieve our goals.

How we can ignore the warnings of Scripture and continue to use honors for manipulation and continue to clamor for them is a dangerously unanswered question.

The teaching of Jesus is very clear about the things we do for the view of others:

"Be careful not to do your 'acts of righteousness' before men, to be seen by them. If you do, you will have no reward from your Father in heaven. So when you give to the needy, do not announce it with trumpets, as the hypocrites do in the synagogues and on the streets, to be honored by men. I tell you the truth, they have received their reward in full." (Matthew 6:1-2)

Jesus invites us to secret giving and, a few sentences later, to secret praying so that the Father is free to reward us openly. It must, however, be left to the Father to handle the reward, not to the hands of men. We cannot rationalize, once we have become part of a self-honoring system, that it comes from the Father because the system honored us and not we ourselves. Paul draws the demarcation line firmly in 2 Corinthians 10:17-18: "But, 'Let him who boasts boast in the Lord.' For it is not the man who commends himself who is approved, but the man whom the Lord commends."

Two instances in which Jesus was apparently given commendation do not provide adequate reason for our own systems of commendation. Luke 2:52 says "Jesus grew . . . in favor with . . . men." However, these same people in whose favor he grew were the very ones who later scoffed at him and rejected him, causing Jesus to state that a prophet was not without honor except in his own country. Later, in the triumphal entry passage of Matthew 21, the crowd that honored him with the palms and "hosannas" also called for his crucifixion. The honors of men, no matter how obtained, are empty and fickle.

The only prize legitimate for us to seek, the only prize that will not be brought low is the ". . . prize of the high calling of God in Christ Jesus," (Philippians 3:14 KJV). That "high calling" is the call to servanthood.

When the Inn Is Full

It isn't that *least* is the cellar in which the indolent, inadequate, apathetic riffraff justly find themselves collected. In the nature of Jesus, *least* is a choice you make when you have such a high view of others that you want to do all you can to elevate them and your position happens, because of your efforts in their behalf, to end up least . . . and you really didn't notice.

Very few people can make it to the top in this world. Some are injured, some are discouraged. But even if all were able, there is so little room at the top that even capable, deserving ones will be thwarted. The inn called fame and fortune is always filled just at the time when you thought you could make it. So many applicants for the best jobs; prices so high for the best housing — there just isn't room.

But there is a place where adequate room seems available. It is called a manger. It is small and dirty and inhabited by animals, but it is the place where the Son of God, the greatest in the kingdom, the servant, was born. And there seems to be enough room when it comes to servanthood. Not many people are fighting to get into the manger. If you really love people and want to serve them, there will always be room. Perhaps no human glory or prizes, but plenty of room.

Mary, when she heard from the angel that she was to bear the Messiah, understood about the proud and the humble and, perhaps even then, about mangers. And Mary said:

> "My soul praises the Lord
>   and my spirit rejoices in God my
>   Savior,
> for he has been mindful of the humble
>   state of his servant.
> From now on all generations will call
>   me blessed,
>   for the Mighty One has done great
>   things for me —
>   holy is his name.
> His mercy extends to those who fear
>   him,
>   from generation to generation.
> He has performed mighty deeds with
>   his arm;
>   he has scattered those who are
>   proud in their inmost thoughts.
> He has brought down rulers from
>   their thrones
>   but has lifted up the humble.
> He has filled the hungry with good
>   things
>   but has sent the rich away empty.
> He has helped his servant Israel,

remembering to be merciful
to Abraham and his descendants
    forever,
even as he said to our fathers."

                                    Luke 1:46-55

So, we find Jesus in humble places — in mangers, among the poor, being a servant, being humble, being an example, being as a child, being as the younger, being as the last and as the least. And wherever he is, his servant will be.

Your attitude should be the same as
that of Christ Jesus:

Who, being in very nature God,

did not consider equality with God

something to be grasped,

but made himself nothing, taking the very

nature of a servant,

being made in human likeness.

And being found in appearance as a man, he

humbled himself

and became obedient to death —

even death on a cross!

Therefore God exalted him to the highest place

and gave him the name that is above every name,

that at the name of Jesus every knee should bow,

in heaven and on earth and under the earth,

and every tongue confess that Jesus Christ is Lord,

to the glory of God the Father.

Philippians 2:5-11

Good-bye Strong Arm Tactics

Christ Jesus . . . did not consider equality with God something to be grasped

Paul delves deeply into the person and nature of Jesus in the letter to the church at Philippi. He uses some of the same descriptions Jesus gave himself in the greatest in the kingdom teachings. But he also adds some fresh insight: "Your attitude should be the same as that of Christ Jesus: Who, being in very nature God, did not consider equality with God something to be grasped" (Philippians 2:5-6). In the simplest interpretation of this passage, it states that though he deserved it, being equal with God, Jesus did not try to take over the kingdom by force.

Major amounts of money are being spent in the world today for armaments, but Jesus valued people too highly to violate them through the use of force. Certainly he had the power to call legions of angels to rescue him from the cross and wreak vengeance on the crowd that had mistreated him. But he didn't.

Certainly he could have roamed the countryside grabbing people by the neck and threatening them with cosmic annihilation if they did not follow him. But he didn't. He refuses to do anything that would destroy or inhibit our ability to choose. Love works that way.

Matthew quotes Isaiah to show the gentleness of Jesus:

> "Here is my servant whom I have
>   chosen,
>   the one I love, in whom I delight;
> I will put my Spirit on him,
>   and he will proclaim justice to the
>   nations.
> He will not quarrel or cry out;
>   no one will hear his voice in the
>   streets.
> A bruised reed he will not break,
>   and a smoldering wick he will not
>   snuff out,
> till he leads justice to victory.
>   In his name the nations will put
>   their hope."
>
>   Matthew 12:18-21

We do not have a comparable idiom for the reference to a bruised reed and a smoldering wick. The closest meaning we can obtain from what he is saying is that "He won't kick a man when he is down and he looks for the slightest spark of hope in people and tries to fan it into flame."

When I was in Boy Scouts, we made fire from flints or from rubbing sticks together. We would take a handful of very flammable material called tinder and place it where sparks from the flint could fall into it or heat from the sticks would make it begin to smolder.

Quick action would soon have a spark in the tinder. I never saw anyone look at that single spark and in disgust stomp it out complaining all the while that it was only one spark. To the contrary, they would pick up the tinder, cup it in their hands and blow through it in an effort to provide additional oxygen and create a flame. That seems so descriptive of the way Jesus treats us and so unlike the way that we treat each other.

As a college teacher I am called upon to evaluate people through grades. It is my least favorite thing about teaching. According to the system, if people do not measure up to at least sixty-five percent of my standard, they are not worthy to be in my continued presence. They must go elsewhere.

Unfortunately, conscious or unconscious grading occurs in our general evaluation of people. If they do not meet a majority of our criteria for quality people, then we do not bother to give them further opportunity to be our friend. In church, if someone does not succeed in living up to our tenets of minimum behavior at least eighty percent of the time, then we no longer have time for such a person.

How different is Jesus' gentle invitation from the condemnatory harangues — voiced or silent — I have heaped upon weary and burdened people: "Come to me, all you who are weary and burdened, and I will give you rest. Take my yoke upon you and learn from me, for I am gentle and humble in heart, and you will find rest for your souls. For my yoke is easy and my burden is light." He does not stamp on us because there is only one spark of hope in us. No, he gently lifts us and blows the great wind of God on us until his fire baptizes us.

Does the End Justify the Means?

The other meaning (additional, not alternate) of Philippians 2:5-6, which speaks of not grasping the kingdom, is that Jesus was not driven by blind ambition. When goals are of the highest order and represent eternal values, keeping the method of achieving those goals in proper balance is difficult. We have all heard the question, "Does the end justify the means?"

Surely Jesus, who had the highest of goals, should have been free to use whatever means he needed to attain the goal; however, he refused to be blindly driven. Anyone who has worked within the ranks of industry or any human economic system is acquainted with the cutthroat methods used by the ambitious to rise in the ranks or to multiply income. Such increase usually comes at the expense of another. In the church, too, people become pawns and stepping stones to others' goals, even very acceptable goals like evangelism.

Winning Ways

Much evangelism is akin to the frenzied eating of a starved shark. We thrash around and produce a lot of blood, thereby fulfilling our hunger for statistics. There is a thought pattern which goes. "The important thing is to get them to say the sinners' prayer. It doesn't matter much how we get them to do it, the important thing is that they do. It doesn't matter if they understand very well what they have done, the important thing is that they do it."

Consequently, we have used every kind of approach to reach sinners short of loving and relating to them. We are taught to approach them as a salesman would, not revealing our reason for the conversation until the right psychological time, and then moving in for the "close" whether there is an invitation for it or not. Then, the ritual concluded, we leave appropriate literature and fade away from the person's life. We leave our new child and hope he finds his way to someone's doorstep or that someone else will remember to visit him.

The only thing akin to a modern altar call in the New Testament occurred on the Day of Pentecost after Peter's sermon when three thousand accepted Christ. The significant difference is that Peter did not issue the call, the crowd did. How different from today! Whether the Holy Spirit moves people or not is immaterial — we try to do it on our own. Evangelists trade secrets of how best to move the greatest number of people to the altar. Having been in the church all my life, I think I have been subjected to all the manipulative forms and it hurts to rethink them, but let's look at a few.

How often I heard closings to sermons that were totally unrelated to the message that had just been given. Instead, a well-placed deathbed story designed only to elicit emotions immediately preceded the call to the front.

The whole structure of heads bowed, eyes closed, the organ gently playing creates an unreal atmosphere that can be destructive to a person's ability to make a genuine choice. In this mood-setting atmosphere, psychological forces unrelated to the choice at hand can come into play and confuse the issue.

Once, when I was presenting the good news to a person and giving him the opportunity to make a decision about Christ, he asked me a question that stopped me in my tracks and made me wonder what kind of grinder he had been through before. He asked me, "Will you still be my friend if I say no?"

Evangelism in the Jesus style never violates or is disrespectful of the freedom of anyone. It increases their ability to make a choice rather than takes it away from them.

Evangelism in the Jesus style never uses deceptive means or dishonesty in any form to make converts. God is truth and reality. Any means that requires that the person be tricked or fooled or any means that works only under a cloud of secrecy is a violation of the Jesus style.

Evangelism in the Jesus style focuses on the person

of Jesus himself rather than any fringe church doc-
trines or styles.

Evangelism in the Jesus style grows out of the fruit
of our lives and asks us to be willing to reveal our
selves, even to sinners.

Again, Jesus, who came to redeem people — not
use them, refused to take advantage of others on his
path to the cross. He easily could have taken advantage of a repentant Zaccheus or of a seeking young
man who was rich or of the crowd he fed who wanted
to make him king. But Jesus, dedicated to the greatest
goal, was equally dedicated to the greatest means.
He was driven by love and obedience, not blind
ambition.

Hello, I'm Reverend . . .

Christ Jesus . . . made himself nothing

He made himself nothing, emptied himself — the great *kenosis*. He made himself of no reputation, no image.

I can recall my father shaking his head and repeating over and over to himself, "If only I knew what this meant. There is something powerful here. If only I understood it." Maybe that is why this Scripture has glued itself to my mind and equally disturbs me. Reputation is so important to me. I want to be seen with the right people, remembered in the right light, advertised with my name spelled right, live in the right neighborhood, drive the right kind of car, wear the right kind of clothing. But Jesus made himself of no reputation!

Image building is a significant industry in the United States. Presidential candidates and others who need a tangible expression of approval from the

113

public spend millions of dollars on simply building their image. Advertising companies spend billions just to let you know that their clients are around and to build an image that will cause you to trust them regardless of the quality of their product. For Americans, image is of supreme importance.

Image or reputation is simply a means to gain control over others or manipulate them to our best advantage. Most people are guilty of it. Certainly we clergymen are. If I were to introduce myself to you by saying, "Hello, I am the Reverend Mister Gayle Dean Erwin," immediately I would have you intimidated. You would clean up your act — quit cursing, hide certain reading material — become unreal.

Or, if I don't get to introduce myself, I can wear a black suit and white shirt and immediately you know I am either an umpire, undertaker, or a preacher. Same result.

Or I can simply speak with my pulpit voice, the sanctuary tone with a tear in every word, and immediately you know only preachers talk that way. Once again, I have you cowed.

In an airplane between Los Angeles and Dallas, I had occasion to share the good news with the owner of an electronics manufacturing company. As he neared the point at which he would accept the Lord, he stopped and asked me what I did for a living. I told him I was a minister. The wheels began turning in his head as he wondered what he had been saying to this clergyman. A lady seated on the other side of me, overhearing that I was a clergyman, squealed with delight and asserted that she had wanted to meet one so she could ask him some questions. Whereupon, she asked me something like how many angels can actually sit on the head of a pin. The conversation with the executive then became "proper." The weight of all the unreal image we have helped to build came crashing down on me.

I still wonder at the books I have read, written by great men, that urge me to keep up a professional image as a minister. They exhort me not to let my people get close to me or see me with my hair down or call me by my first name. They must be taught to respect the office of pastor and honor it as a profession, so these books tell me. Perhaps that is why I meet so many lonely, frustrated pastors in my travels. But God has not designed us to live that way. And according to Luke, Jesus didn't live that way either: "Now the tax collectors and 'sinners' were all gathering around to hear him. But the Pharisees and the teachers of the law muttered, 'This man welcomes sinners and eats with them' " (Luke 15:1-2).

Jesus kept doing the things that were detrimental to his reputation. He didn't mind who he was seen with. A former prostitute kept constant company with his group. He would do whatever would serve the best interest of a person, regardless of the cost to himself:

Now one of the Pharisees invited Jesus to have dinner with him, so he went to the Pharisee's house and reclined at the table. When a woman who had lived a sinful life in that town learned that Jesus was eating at the Pharisee's house, she brought an alabaster jar of perfume, and as she stood behind him at his feet weeping, she began to wet his feet with her tears. Then she wiped them with her hair, kissed them and poured perfume on them.

When the Pharisee who had invited him saw this, he said to himself, "If this man were a prophet, he would know who is touching him and what kind of woman she is — that she is a sinner." (Luke 7:36-39)

A good Pharisee would never have let a woman, especially one like this, even touch him in public. But in this scene, a woman of ill repute begins to caress the feet of Jesus in the only way her skills had taught her to do. Rather than rebuke her for it, Jesus rebukes the judgmental Pharisee and honors this repentant woman who had kissed his feet ceaselessly from the time Jesus arrived.

I have a friend in a large foreign city where prostitution is legal and the women display themselves in rooms so customers can make a choice of who they want. He is a respected pastor whom God has burdened with the plight of these women. He realized that no one cared about them. Anyone who could have helped them avoided the place where they were so as not to tarnish their own reputation. He began to enter these houses and talk with the women there. At first they tried to be erotic, but quickly they realized that he was not there to take advantage of their bodies and began to talk with him about Christ and reality. This pastor risks all of his reputation and image for such a burden of love. I suspect Jesus did the same.

If I am but a pilgrim and stranger in this world, I do not need to hold on to anything that would guarantee my success in it, not my reputation, and not my possessions either.

Possessions Are Nine Tenths . . .

Paul gives us further insight in 2 Corinthians 8:9 into what it meant for Jesus to make himself nothing: "For you know the grace of our Lord Jesus Christ, that though he was rich, yet for your sakes he became poor, so that you through his poverty might become rich."

Whether we interpret this to be poor in spirit or poor in finances, the outcome is a major shaking of our own nature. After gaining new insight into the nature of Jesus, I can begin to understand why he said that it is more difficult for a rich man to enter the kingdom of heaven than for a camel to go through the eye of a needle. Possessing wealth is probably the strongest deterrent to growing into the nature and lifestyle of Jesus. A wealthy man has so much to give up.

When Jesus talked to the rich young ruler, who had put honest effort into right living and thinking, and discerned that he was possessed by his riches, the final instructions were "go and sell what you have and give it to the poor."

I have been fascinated by how many people (including me) rationalize their desire to be wealthy by stating that they wished to be rich so they could help people with their money. Meanwhile, they gave themselves to no ministry that indicated even a slight desire to serve people.

Ah, yes, Jesus knew the hearts of men and he knew how best to resist temptation for himself as well. His instructions were not, "go and sell what you have and give it to God through my organization." Nor were they, "Show your love and devotion by selling what you have and giving it to me, the Lord."

The rich young ruler seemed to have everything else correct. Perhaps fulfilling Jesus' instructions was the only step he lacked in being able to become a lover of people. Yet, apparently Jesus did not say to all of the wealthy friends he had that they must sell all and give to the poor as he did to the rich young ruler. He has a keen sense of where our treasure and heart is.

Jesus did not pull back from the total impact of what he had to say about wealth even though it was not always understood by the disciples and was especially not appreciated by the Pharisees. The Pharisees felt that their possession of things was a sign that God was pleased with them and that people were poor because it was a sign of God's displeasure. Jesus consistently reversed the value systems of the world:

> The Pharisees, who loved money, heard all this and were sneering at Jesus. He said to them, "You are the ones who justify your-

selves in the eyes of men, but God knows your
hearts. What is highly valued among men is
detestable in God's sight." (Luke 16:14-15)

Men's value: God's abomination. What an indictment of our system!
The nature of Jesus, however, is both opposite to
the fallen nature of man and redemptive of it. Jesus
gives us insight into the proper priority of values in
the following conversation:

"Teacher, we know that you speak and
teach what is right, and that you do not show
partiality but teach the way of God in accor-
dance with the truth. Is it right for us to pay
taxes to Caesar or not?"
He saw through their duplicity and said to
them, "Show me a denarius. Whose portrait
and inscription are on it?"
"Caesar's," they replied.
He said to them, "Then give to Caesar what
is Caesar's, and to God what is God's." (Luke
20:21-25)

Money falls under the realm of Caesar's whether it
says "In God we trust" on it or not. It is the stuff of
this world — the symbol around which our greed
gathers.
In this age, the desire for "more" has led parents to
take multiple jobs in order to provide their families
with higher standards of living. In this drive to excel,
they have deprived their children of the richest of

gifts — themselves. I pray for a generation that will accept a lesser standard of living in order to give themselves away to their families and others.

People are the realm of God. His inscription is on us. He has created us in his image and we are to be given to him. His making himself poor was not to create a dramatic show and thus impress the world or simply prove to himself that he could do it. No, he made himself poor for our benefit — so that by his poverty we might be made rich.

Building Bigger Barns

It is easy to lose sight of proper priorities in the practical decisions of life. For example, take the choices that we must make regarding church buildings. Church facilities as we know them were not part of the early church and certainly were not commanded by Jesus. They are made compatible with the nature of Jesus only by diligent awareness and effort.

When we decide on the location for a building, we have made a sociological decision as to which strata of people will feel comfortable coming to it. Then, when we decide on the architectural style, we have made another sociological decision as to who will feel comfortable being present in it. Each choice reduces the number of people. When we choose the liturgy we will use, we have made another sociological decision as to who will worship with us. Our choice of clothing style, reading material and rules and regulations limits even further who will attend.

The whole approach of Jesus seems to be to remove those limits. He opened his arms to the weary and heavy laden. Anything we do that in any way closes the door to that group is out of step with the nature of Jesus.

One of the most powerful abominations that has crept into our decision process concerning church facilities is the statement, "Jesus deserves the best." I agree that he does, but the problem is that we haven't the foggiest idea what the best is until we thoroughly understand and pursue the nature of Jesus. Otherwise we will attempt to foist material opulence on him who avoided exactly such self-glorification. I think that what we are saying is, "We deserve the best."

How have we so perverted the gospel that we concentrate the majority of our church income on the facilities instead of on the people? The world stands up and cries, "Selfish!" If we are truly pilgrims passing through this world, what purpose is served in spending so much of our time, energy and resources on a physical building while the needs of people go untouched?

If we are locked into a building or building program, then we need to ask certain questions of it. Will it enable us to be better slaves? Will it cause us to lord it over others? What will we be examples of in this building? Can we be humble here? Can we be as a child in this building? Is this building a product of our ambition? If we had to pay for it individually, would we still do it? Would people think we had made ourselves of no reputation with this building? Would we die for this building or is it expendable? What will we do to keep people from damaging this building? Will we let them stain the carpet? Will we permit bare feet here? Would those bare feet be comfortable here anyway? Are there any furnishings that memorialize persons other than Christ? Are there any pews or areas that are "understood" to be reserved for certain people? In what ways can we tell the difference between the rich and the poor in this building?

If we must have buildings, then let us break away from the theater designs of the last centuries in which the performance on the stage is the most important thing and all seats are fixed in that direction. Let us begin to design buildings that will enhance the interaction of the body and give us a chance to fulfill the call to love one another. Let it be known that the congregation is where the action is and God, not our structure, is the center of worship. Let us drop the Saturday marquee page in the newspaper that tells what performance is going on where in our efforts to lure fish away from another fishbowl.

Whatever buildings we have, let us utilize them fully seven days a week so as to be good stewards. And whatever we build, let us hold to it ever so lightly, knowing that those things that can be shaken will be shaken, causing only the permanent to remain.

Down to Earth

Taking the very nature of a servant,
being made in human likeness.
And being found in appearance as a man

A church administrator in a high position once expressed that he feared I was describing Jesus in terms too human. He felt that it was dangerously close to humanism. Hardly. Humanism recognizes no divine other than mankind. But Jesus was fully God, fully man. If he was fully man, then he was just like me, a man with the same passions and temptations that I have.

The writer of Hebrews reveals to us that: "We do not have a high priest who is unable to sympathize with our weaknesses, but we have one who has been tempted in every way, just as we are — yet was without sin" (Hebrews 4:15).

Tempted in every way just as I am? The Son of God? That is a little hard to believe, but it is so. Occasionally, I believe that I have original temptations — ones that Jesus could never possibly have faced, but he did.

James writes that, "Each one is tempted when, by his own evil desire, he is dragged away and enticed" (James 1:14).

Does this mean that the lust structure of Jesus was like mine? Apparently so, for that is the source of temptation, when we are drawn away of our own lusts. Yet he was without sin. It encourages me that though he was just like me, he was able to perfectly obey his Father and now imparts that ability as well as his sinlessness to me. Fully human — sweating, smelling, bathing, eliminating. Fully human, fully God.

This frees me to be humble, to own my own humanity, to not try to hide it in the presence of friends, not try to put on a mask of spirituality if it is not there, to learn to be honest about myself, to be free to be forgiven, and to forgive.

Living Without Weights

Nothing is quite as regular as paying the bills. Most of us never escape the burden of our debts though we long to be free. In the same way, by the time we reach age thirty, we can record a long list of things we wish we hadn't said or done — trespasses against others for which we carry the burden of guilt. And also by age thirty, we can list injustices we have suffered whose memories awaken anger in us, adding bitterness to our burden.

The burdens of debt, trespasses and bitterness are all weights that destroy our peace and our right relationship with others — weights that can only be removed by forgiveness. Servanthood knows that bitterness cripples the slave and renders him useless, and servanthood wants for others the freedom that comes from forgiveness. Jesus chose forgiveness as a major trait of those who follow him:

> Then Peter came to Jesus and asked, "Lord, how many times shall I forgive my brother when he sins against me? Up to seven times?" Jesus answered, "I tell you, not seven times, but seventy-seven times." (Matthew 18:21-22)

Usually, I am good for three times of forgiveness, although I am cautious after the first time. But Jesus wants me to identify with the struggling brother who desires to change but can't always get it together. Jesus wants me to teach him how to forgive by forgiving, just as he taught the disciples by saying, "Father forgive them, for they do not know what they are doing."

It is as if Jesus, in spite of the horrendous scars and deep wounds we had given him, conspired with the Father to get even with us and said, "Let's teach them a lesson. Let's forgive them." God help me to love the sinner in his sin and let him know it! Sin is a distortion of our created nature. Forgiveness has an amazing power to correct that distortion.

Forgiveness also has a way of eliminating the distance between people, bringing us close enough to touch and embrace — actions very much in keeping with servanthood.

Love Wrapped in Skin

Few things communicate acceptance and warmth to us as much as touch. Even a child knows its value. One night a mother went into her little girl's bedroom to comfort her in the midst of a thunderstorm. The mother said, "Don't worry; Jesus is here and he will protect you." Her daughter responded, "Okay, you sleep here with Jesus and I will go sleep with daddy!" That child wanted touch!

It seems so appropriate that the incarnation would bring to us the servant king who would touch us and let us touch him. Scripture is filled with references to Jesus touching. Since his love for mankind is so complete, even the lepers, the untouchables, felt the warmth of his hands. Children, animals, the ground he created were all beneficiaries of his touch. Little wonder that so many of the "one anothers" of the New Testament express an intimacy that would require touch. Little wonder that the touch of washing feet was a requirement for fellowship between Jesus and Peter. Little wonder that touch (even of a garment hem) provides such healing. Little wonder, then, that the ordaining of ministries requires the "laying on of hands." Little wonder that gifts and birthrights were passed along by the laying on of hands. Little wonder that the writer of Hebrews considered the doctrine of the laying on of hands to be elementary.

Jesus was even vulnerable to touch. In the garden after his resurrection, he tells Mary Magdalene not to keep on touching him since he had not yet ascended to the Father. Evidently her female caresses were too potent for him as long as he was still in the flesh.

While on earth, Jesus was love wrapped in skin! And even now, the saga of the incarnation continues as Jesus serves us in advocacy before the Father. The book of Hebrews reminds us that he is still touched with the feeling of our infirmities (4:15).

Like Father, Like Son

He humbled himself and became obedient

Obedience has always had a distorted meaning in my mind. For me, it represented an unwelcome taskmaster, a demand that you do what you didn't want to do and maybe didn't think was right, and that you were made to do by someone larger and stronger than yourself. This does not seem to be the meaning of obedience in the life of Christ. What was the difference?

Obedience was a joy for him because it was being true to the original nature, the made-in-the-image-of-God nature, that Adam and Eve had polluted by their choices. The special mark of Jesus' life was his total obedience to his Father: "I tell you the truth, the Son can do nothing by himself; he can do only what he sees his Father doing, because whatever the Father does the Son also does. For the Father loves the Son and shows him all he does" (John 5:19-20).

Since Jesus was revealing the nature of God, then we must assume that the traits discussed in these pages describe the God of all creation. God and his Son are servants, examples, humble, as a child, as the younger, as the last, as the least, using no force, emptying themselves. These traits that totally speak love were guiding principles, even commands, for the life of Jesus. He was completely faithful to them.

Jesus was obedient to this servant love of man even in Gethsemane when the cost was going up astronomically. At the most crucial point, he chose to do the act that would most lovingly display the reality of the Father to us.

In my own selfishness I usually fail at that very point — my ability to make choices always loving of others. But Jesus knew the secret of obedience which produces joy. In Matthew he gives to his disciples what may be the most condensed secret of God, the atom out of which all else is built:

> "If anyone would come after me, he must deny himself and take up his cross and follow me. For whoever wants to save his life will lose it, but whoever loses his life for me will find it." (Matthew 16:24-25)

If I could put this principle fully into effect in my life, all the others being discussed here would fall into place. This is the essence of how God operates, the essence of what holds the universe together, the essence of what keeps my body going, the essence of what keeps the body of Christ functioning; so to activate it in my life unlocks the power of God for me more than anything else. It isn't mysterious or mystical at all. But it doesn't have the drama behind it that other verses do, so it is easy for me to neglect. Working on the principle of giving myself away has provided greater results in counseling for me than any other principle. It has drastically altered my own life. All the selfish forces that create the abnormalities and sufferings of life fall by the wayside when I get in touch with the God-life, the atom that moves me to act in love toward others.

The charismatic gifts around which so much excitement revolves are also subject to this principle. None of them are to be used for self-seeking purposes — only for the edification of the body. The ministry gifts are to be used for the equipping of others. Any act not beneficial to others is disobedient and damaging to the body.

Our piety has been polluted, with many of our holiness requirements becoming purely personal and having little to do with how we relate to others.

At a Christian festival, I had a conversation with two couples, one of whom was Buddhist, in response to a session I had taught in the afternoon. About halfway through the conversation, the Christian man lit a cigarette, then apologized, saying he wanted to give them up because they hurt his witness.

The Buddhist woman responded with a statement that continues to shake me. She said, "We non-Christians, when one of our rank becomes a Christian, do not watch them to see how well they live up to some self-imposed standard of piety. We watch them to see how they start treating people." I felt as if I had heard the word of the Lord from her. The Pharisees could accuse Jesus of being a glutton and a winebibber, but they could not accuse him of not loving people. He had succeeded. He had been obedient to his Father.

A Strange Catchword

Power for obedience to the Father came to Jesus by the anointing of the Spirit that comes from the Father. Anointing, however, is not always clearly understood. In the past I have heard it used as a strange catchword. When a minister felt that he had the *anointing*, the physical results were immediate. The voice rose in volume. Pulpit pounding would increase. Similarly, when a congregation talked of a preacher who was anointed, it had nothing to do with what he was saying, but instead was a way of describing the style with which he preached.

But let us see what the anointing does to Jesus. First, he is driven into the desert by the Spirit where, while fasting, he is tempted heavily by the devil. There he sees the strength of the things that make us fall. He perceives what we go through and discovers how much of dust we are. Then, with the battle won, he goes to the synagogue where a scroll from Isaiah is handed to him and he reads:

"The Spirit of the Lord is on me,
   because he has anointed me
   to preach good news to the poor.
He has sent me to proclaim freedom
   for the prisoners
   and recovery of sight for the blind,
to release the oppressed,
   to proclaim the year of the Lord's
   favor."

Luke 4:18-19

That is what the anointing did to Jesus. It caused him to fulfill his nature — to be obedient.

Sacred anointing, as different from social or medicinal anointing, has a specific meaning — to dedicate to God, to set apart, to empower for a specific purpose. The word *Messiah*, or *Christ*, means "the anointed one." In other words, Jesus was fully dedicated, fully set apart, fully empowered, not to some volume of voice or manner of eloquence, but to *do* something — to preach good news, to proclaim freedom, to give sight, and to release. That is what the anointing must produce in me if I follow in his steps.

Along with what the anointing caused him to do, notice the clientele to which it sent him — poor, prisoners, blind, oppressed — hardly the most attractive sort of companions. None of these people would be able to properly repay him for his services. They could only receive. Obedience thinks more about giving than receiving.

Let us see the kind of people our anointing will send us to and what we are to say to them.

Whose Side Is God On?

Good news to the poor. I think I would more likely want to preach good news to the rich. The returns are better. But poor people hardly know what to do with good news; they seldom get any. They tend to go overboard when something good comes along and take advantage of it. You can't help the poor until they understand better how to handle being helped, I tend to think. But the first result of the anointing of Jesus was to give the poor good news.

Freedom for the prisoners. When is the last time you visited someone in jail? You may be a little ashamed if you even know someone who is in jail.

If, like me, you are apt to say, "Why should I visit someone in jail? They are there because of the wheels of justice, and part of their punishment and rehabilitation is to be deprived of interaction with people like me," then this part of the anointing has meaning that is deeply disturbing.

Not all people in jails received or are receiving justice. Many of them, because they have no wealth to keep the legal processes going, are swiftly forgotten and, long past the time they should have been released had justice been dished out equally, languish in a cell. Prisons are great places for individuals to be forgotten. That is certainly not healthy for a person's outlook on life. So Jesus finds the forgotten and remembers them.

Though they have failed society and are paying debts, the fact remains that those in prisons are people, and Jesus came for people. After imprisonment for his role in Watergate, Chuck Colson, as a legal expert, saw the unjust situation of so many in prisons. This revelation so changed his attitudes that he has now gone from being a presidential advisor to a minister to prisoners in the name of Jesus.

Prisons are not the best neighborhood for developing a strong personality and high self-image; yet that is our goal for others if we love them. Jesus did, so he came to proclaim freedom for the prisoners.

If you are uncomfortable with my emphasis on literal prisons and prefer to see that in the context of spiritual prisons, the analogy is still appropriate. Much of the world is captive to some addiction — drugs, alcohol, tobacco, gambling, perversion — or locked into inappropriate emotional reactions. We often isolate such prisoners as surely as if they were behind bars. We yell at them through their bars or from a distance to tell them that they are free, but show no indication that we really believe they are by giving the gift of our presence.

Prisoners of sin and prisoners behind walls also suffer the stigma of being viewed with suspicion and seldom trusted once they are released. Once we begin to minister to them we will find that they take immense amounts of our time and energy. I guess we will have to be lovers of people and anointed before we will ever proclaim freedom to prisoners.

Recovery of sight for the blind. One of my running arguments with God is that not enough people are healed to please me. His running argument with me is that I both fail to pray for them enough and fail to walk with them through their recovery. Healing is something I don't understand. I have seen enough of it to believe that it occurs and is not always psychologically explainable. But I have also seen enough to know that the pop theologies which clobber the sheep for not having enough faith are inadequate. When Jesus walked the earth, he healed the sick freely. In some places he healed all the sick. I doubt that the faith of those crowds exceeded that of today. Only occasionally did Jesus compliment outstanding faith, yet he continued to heal. The only places he didn't do much healing was where *dis*belief was the major attitude.

When hurting people come to Jesus today and ask for people to pray for them, it is not out of disbelief that they have come. Some are healed, but not all. To send away the unhealed, who came in belief, with a condemning sermon on their lack of faith ringing in their ears does not sound like Jesus to me. I do not understand why some are healed and others are not, but I am under orders from the Master Servant, so I will pray for the sick (and blind) and leave the healing up to the Lord. In the meantime, what is my ministry to the blind (physically or spiritually) as they recover? I can walk with them, keep them on the road and away from harm, talk to them to restore their personhood, and keep them constantly in touch with the Healer. If you will forgive my selfishness, I enjoy being the first one a physically or spiritually blind person actually sees.

"To release the oppressed" (NIV) — *"To set at liberty them that are bruised"* (KJV). Oppressed people are an enigma to us. We want to help them but they keep doing things that frighten us and often they throw our help right back into our face. So we end up believing that they are oppressed because they deserve to be.

Whether or not they deserve it, the heart of the church should always beat in harmony with the heart of the oppressed. Often it doesn't. Even worse, the greatest of abominations occur when the church is a source of oppression. To exclude anyone because of his color or station in life or to support, as a church, institutions that do is totally out of step with the nature of Jesus. It is not listening to the Father. It is a sin that removes the action of the Holy Spirit from us. I only hope that it doesn't involve holding Jesus up to such shame that it falls within the category of the unpardonable.

Many of us in the church missed a golden opportunity during the 1960s as radicals took up the cause of the oppressed. I don't care whether the radicals had a hidden agenda or used the wrong methods or not. We should have been with them in our desire to free the oppressed. We should have been there first. Instead, because we didn't like the radicals, we used them as the reason we didn't release the oppressed. Then, we decided that anyone who tried to release the oppressed was probably just like those radicals and was undoubtedly Communist inspired. Jesus didn't care who else was on the side of the oppressed. He only knew that he was. I think I try to protect my reputation too much. Maybe I should empty myself just as he did.

The other side of the coin is the releasing of those personally bruised and oppressed persons. When someone hits us, it will likely leave a bruise. Because of the potential pain, we try to protect bruised spots on our body. Additional bruises cause us to take additional steps to protect ourselves until, finally, we are twisted hulks whose whole lives are wrapped up in attempting to shield our injuries.

After a disappointment in love, I said to myself that I would never let anyone get that close to me again. I even threatened never to love again. Our bruises thus become the starting points at which we begin to cut ourselves off from the vulnerable, loving, person-oriented lifestyle and begin instead to center our lives around self-protection. That is walking death and oppression. Jesus calls us, through the same anointing, to gently find and heal the bruises so people can be free to live without self-protection.

Jesus told us in the gospel of Matthew (7:3-5) not to cast out the splinter from someone else's eye until we have removed the log from our own. This provides a symbol of how we are to help the hurting. I must never approach others as the official splinter hunter. That will only cause them to recoil in fear.

However, if I have had a log removed from my eye, you can be sure that I will remember the pain associated with it and will deal very gently with others who have a splinter. And I would not go myself to an eye doctor who had two logs sticking out from his own eyes.

To proclaim the year of the Lord's favor. What is it about me that wants to let the world know that it is in disfavor with God? Had I been one of the group that caught the woman in the act of adultery, I probably would have scolded her thoroughly and voted for her stoning.

As a young evangelist, I went around telling the world just how evil it was. Of course, it already knew. People's hearts condemn them already. I was saying it more eloquently and forcefully, I thought.

Then I hear Jesus say that the anointing will cause me to proclaim to the world that God is on their side. We are in favor with him. How different it is from my message and yet how much it is the message the world longs to know.

So the work of the Holy Spirit in anointing Jesus was totally consistent with the nature of Jesus and his Father — it resulted in dedication and obedience, in thoroughly giving himself to others and serving them. Will the anointing do any less for me?

Shepherds Don't Run

He humbled himself and became obedient to death — even death on a cross

"Greater love has no one than this, that one lay down his life for his friends" (John 15:13). This is the ultimate test of love. Am I willing to go that far in giving myself away? It is important that we note that Jesus was not coerced into any of this. Love is always a choice. No one is ever forced to love. To be enslaved is one thing, but to choose to serve — that constitutes love. So even the step of death was a loving choice that Jesus made.

"I am the good shepherd. The good shepherd lays down his life for the sheep. The hired hand is not the shepherd who owns the sheep. So when he sees the wolf coming, he abandons the sheep and runs away. Then the wolf attacks the flock and scatters it. The man runs away because he is a hired hand and cares nothing for the sheep.

"I am the good shepherd; I know my sheep and my sheep know me — just as the Father knows me and I know the Father — and I lay down my life for the sheep. I have other sheep that are not of this sheep pen. I must bring them also. They too will listen to my voice, and there shall be one flock and one shepherd. The reason my Father loves me is that I lay down my life — only to take it up again. No one takes it from me, but I lay it down of my own accord. I have authority to lay it down and authority to take it up again. This command I received from my Father." (John 10:11-18)

Power for such self-giving can only come from knowing what the Father is like and hearing his voice. The important response now is for his sheep to hear his voice, to know what kind of sounds the Father makes, to hear the call of the servant nature, to understand that obedience to him means never to violate others by being self-serving. Jesus knew that death did not end it all — it merely began a whole new world.

Serendipity

Therefore God exalted him

Examining the nature of Jesus as we have leaves the natural me a little afraid. None of these traits of the man Jesus are useful to conquer the world, yet Jesus left us with the command to make disciples of all nations. How, without using power, influence and money can we make his name known? How can such a nonself-serving system ever get the job done?

Here, God reveals the bottom line to this list of the traits of Jesus. He lets us know where his interests lie. In the Philippians 2 passage, Paul gives the results of living the Jesus nature of obedience to the Father:

> Therefore God exalted him to the
>   highest place
> and gave him the name that is
>   above every name,
> that at the name of Jesus every knee
>   should bow,

in heaven and on earth and under
the earth,
and every tongue confess that Jesus
Christ is Lord,
to the glory of God the Father.
Philippians 2:9-11

Now I see. If we live after God's manner, we will get God's results. We cannot win the world in our own strength, so we must approach it in a way that frees God to use his power in our behalf.

I have seen people succeed in religious circles who did not use much of the Jesus style. This disturbed me until I saw it in perspective. Their success was minor compared to what it could have been. We can succeed on our own, but the success will be restricted to the limits of our human abilities and will never fully do the job left to us. But when we live in the Jesus style, our success is limited only to God's ability.

It will never fit our worldly logic, but it will fit our faith and will unquestionably require us to trust him, but he is faithful and promises to uphold his part of the deal. He says to us: "I no longer call you servants, because a servant does not know his master's business. Instead, I have called you friends, for everything that I have learned from my Father I have made known to you" (John 15:15).

That is the glorious outcome. Now we know how to pray. Now we know how to love. Now we know the source of power. Now we know how to use power.

The Power Broker

*Jesus knew that the Father had put all things
under his power*

I was watching a television program in which candidates for a certain body-building title were being interviewed. As they walked out onto the stage, the muscles rippled beneath their oiled skins like so many small animals racing each other. Their show of strength was awesome. When the announcer asked them what they did with their strength, their answer was to take appropriate poses to show again the shape of their muscles. The more he insisted on knowing how they used their strength, the more they took poses of power. What do you do when you have all that power?

For the last quarter century, Superman has been part of the American culture. Begun as a comic book, then serialized on television, his adventures have now been made into a series of expensive movies. We are enraptured by the thought of being faster than a speeding bullet, more powerful than a

145

locomotive, able to leap tall buildings with a single bound. We love power and Superman fits our deepest fantasies perfectly. But what do you do with all that power?

What does Jesus do? Jesus knows, in John 13, the time has come. He prepares to show the disciples the "full extent of his love." Jesus is aware that he has come from God and is returning to him, and he knows that the Father has put all things under his power. What are we to expect now? Fireworks? An awesome show of raw power?

Imagine Jesus, biceps bulging beneath a seamless robe with flowing cape, reclining at supper with his disciples. The forces of evil have been collecting for months and are about to kill him, but don't worry, all the power ever created is coursing through his body. He gets up — this man surrounded by overwhelming evil forces — walks over to the disciples and with all this incredible power . . . begins to do what? "He got up from the meal, took off his outer clothing, and wrapped a towel around his waist. After that, he poured water into a basin and began to wash his disciples' feet. . . ." So that is what he does with power! He washes feet.

We do not have a custom with which to compare footwashing. Footwashing was a hospitable thing always done by a slave or the head of the house if he were too poor to have a slave. It was a lowly thing never done by persons of significance for whom it would represent loss of stature. It is like having the president of the United States clean the restrooms of the White House or having a king sweep the streets.

One would not perform such a lowly job and risk losing stature unless he were completely comfortable with his own identity. Jesus knew who he was and consequently didn't have to prove anything. He could do the lowest job.

Had it been me, I would have held one foot slightly elevated for all the disciples to see as I coughed nervously and hinted that something important had been left undone. It would have been beneath me to do such work.

Peter recognized that this behavior was beneath the dignity of Jesus. He was unable to receive such a free gift so he told Jesus that he would not allow his feet to be washed. Jesus' answer speaks volumes about our relationship to him and each other and about his nature: "Unless I wash you, you have no part with me." Unless we understand the true nature of Jesus and let him be to us what he is to be, we can never fully comprehend him or truly be a part of him. We may be a member of his club or take on much of the right vocabulary, but unless he serves us, we have no part or fellowship with him.

Peter's response is typical of the way we approach one another. "Above all, you must not see the real me," we reason. "I will wash my own feet and you can rinse them ritually." Perhaps, just as not letting Jesus wash our feet removes us from fellowship with him, not fulfilling the command of Jesus to wash one another's feet removes us from fellowship with each other. We are to be cleansing agents to each other, removing the dust of our daily travels to prepare us to sit at the table of the Lord.

When he had finished washing their feet, he put on his clothes and returned to his place. "Do you understand what I have done for you?" he asked them.

"You call me 'Teacher' and 'Lord,' and rightly so, for that is what I am. Now that I, your Lord and Teacher, have washed your feet, you also should wash one another's feet. I have set you an example that you should do as I have done for you. I tell you the truth, no servant is greater than his master, nor is a messenger greater than the one who sent him." (John 13:12-16)

Some interpret this passage to mean that Jesus was instituting a new type of ritual, an actual footwashing service. I have no real argument with those who do so. I have been in footwashing services and they can be a time of real exhilaration. However, I have never been in a service where there were any dirty feet. We are careful to clean them thoroughly before we expose them to the gaze, smell and touch of the saints.

Personally, I doubt that Jesus was introducing a new liturgy. He definitely was telling us how we were to relate to one another. If it is not literally to wash feet, then what are we to do to fulfill this commandment? One question in response would be, "What things make us feel cleaner and more fit for the Master's table?"

When someone takes the time to listen to me, I feel as if my feet have been washed. When I am complimented, my feet have been washed. When someone shares a joy with me, my feet have been washed. When someone values my ear enough to share a burden or confess, my feet have been washed. There are countless ways to wash feet. We need only to begin to notice where the dirt comes from in our own lives and we can give cleansing to others.

This thought altered my approach to Sunday sermonizing. I began to realize that neatly dressed people seated neatly in rows are not feeling neat inside. Most of them struggle with non-Christian fellow workers, some listen to constant streams of profanity and off-color stories. Many of the women have been propositioned in the past week. Families sit coolly angry and nonconversant. Guilt, real and unreal, hovers over them and strikes deeply at their inner beings.

Shall I flail them with ominous words from a pulpit? Shall I berate them because they live no better? Shall I blame them for a broken heart? No, they, like me, need their feet washed.

We cannot discover true fellowship until our times together as Christians are footwashing times.

"Now that you know these things, you will be blessed if you do them." (John 13:17)

Living in Style

The Sweet and the Bitter

In following a map, we must first know where we are before we can know where to go. Now that we have seen Jesus and ourselves in contrast, we at least have some idea of where we are. By now it should be obvious that our journey is going to take a lifetime, but we will get there!

When Ezekiel was told, after receiving a revelation from God, to eat the words he had written, he found them to be sweet in his mouth and bitter in his stomach. There is a parallel to that in the words I have shared with you. As good as they may sound or taste, they are difficult to digest simply because they are so opposite to our natural inclinations. We begin to fear and tremble as we work out this salvation.

Thankfully, we have help. We will see that clearly as we look now at the body of Christ and at God's involvement in our personal growth. It will become obvious also that God's invitations have an R.S.V.P. note on them.

The Ankle Bone Connected to the Foot Bone

God has combined the members of the body and has given greater honor to the parts that lacked it, so that there should be no division in the body, but that its parts should have equal concern for each other. If one part suffers, every part suffers with it; if one part is honored, every part rejoices with it.

Now you are the body of Christ, and each one of you is a part of it. (1 Corinthians 12:24-27)

It is appropriate that God chose the body as an analogy for his followers. It is organic, flexible, growing. It can only survive as it lives according to the nature of Jesus. Not one part of the natural body exists for itself. Every single part of the human body is designed and placed there to be a servant to the rest of the body. If a part of the natural body becomes self-centered and begins to exist only for itself, it becomes what medical doctors call cancer. Both my natural body and the body of Christ can survive only as long as each part functions as servant to the rest of the parts.

The analogy of our being a body can be carried to some logical conclusions. No body has any ambitious parts in it. You would never hear my toes say to me, "If I am a really good toe, can I work my way up the body and become a knee, an elbow, or a nose?" Ridiculous! My toes spend most of their lives in darkness. They have been seen by few people. They work under great pressure and in less than the best atmosphere. Yet they do not complain that they have never tasted ice cream or that the face gets more attention. Never once have they said, "If this is all the thanks I get, I'm going to join another body."

If an ankle is sprained and cannot carry its share of the load, the body does not threaten to cut it off because it makes the whole body limp. The other parts of the body are glad that they can take up the slack while the injured part is repaired.

When I am driving a nail and accidentally hit the wrong nail — the one on my thumb — my injured hand does not grab the hammer and beat the other thumb to get even for the injury.

My right hand does not berate my left hand because it is weaker and not as dexterous as my right hand.

Shaving scrapes off a layer of skin that requires the corpuscles of the blood to come and repair it. They do it every day. Not once do they complain that if the person doesn't learn his lesson and quit damaging his face, they will cease healing the shaved area.

My fist does not hit my stomach if it aches or my face if it is burned; quite the opposite. My body is carefully self-protective. Without regard to its own safety, my hand will cover my face to protect the eyes.

Occasionally the parts of my body will signal their complaint if they are overworked, but at no time do I have to handle a stack of complaints from the parts of my body saying they resent the part that they are.

Surely what this all means is obvious. If we are members of the body of Christ, we are designed to serve one another. That is the only way Christ would have it to be.

Prisoners of History

If our individual lives are expected to reflect the nature of Jesus, then the structures we individuals form — our organizations, our denominations — are not in an exempt category. Yet within a few years of the founding of almost all religious groups, they begin to take on the characteristics of the average business corporation. They are shaped like a pyramid in their authority structure. Efficiency experts begin to determine their functions rather than body structure and spiritual gifts. Nepotism reigns; they become ingrown and far removed from the thinking of their constituencies. Corporate proclamations vastly differ from the private expressions of the individual members.

In personal conversations with a number of different persons on high denominational boards, I have found them to be basically progressive men

157

who cared for people and had deep misgivings about various theologies and about their own roles. But when they get into a meeting together, the product of the meeting is opposite to their private expressions. I wonder if they aren't getting their signals from somewhere else once they fall into the system that resembles that of the world. If an organization's system deprives or inhibits persons in their ability to hear from God and decide on that basis, then something is drastically wrong. That is not the Jesus style.

It was the nature of Jesus to be given to persons. It is the nature of organizations to be given to self-preservation. To be self-seeking is to violate the words of Jesus: "Whoever tries to keep his life will lose it, and whoever loses his life will preserve it" (Luke 17:53).

After a period of time, structures begin to suffer "hardening of the categories" and those categories become more important to them than the persons they serve. The Greek myth of Procrustes describes the situation well.

Procrustes had a house midway between two major cities and a day's journey from each. Because of its location, travelers sought it out regularly for a night's lodging and for meals. The hospitality of the home of Procrustes was beyond any that the travelers had ever experienced before. Meals were sumptuous, rooms were spacious. Payment was not accepted. Procrustes allowed them the run of the house and informed them that there were no rules for them to worry about. Only one requirement would be laid upon them for the whole night. Joy abounded. Then the requirement was revealed. Every person who stayed there would have to fit the bed. If he was too short, he would be stretched. If he was too tall, he would be cut off.

Many people fit the bed, slept well, and went about praising the hospitality of Procrustes to their friends in various cities, urging them to spend a night there when they traveled through. But many people died in the house of Procrustes. No one heard their testimony.

When denominations and other religious organizations become established, their theologies and social structures tend to be rigid. Anyone with fresh insight or a prophetic word is stoned verbally or excluded from the Jerusalem (headquarters) of the group. Only those who fit the prescribed pattern survive. Also, as systems of choosing personnel are refined, only those who can move up through the ranks are accepted. Spiritual leadership falls by the wayside as the rigid bed of political ability wins. The early days of most new movements are marked by outstanding leadership, often chosen because it simply is outstanding. Later, as the movement dies, leadership in the resulting institution follows a more bureaucratic model.

On several occasions I have asked people who were training for ministry to list the persons to whom they looked for spiritual leadership in the church. Never has an elected official of any organization been named. Somehow, the rights to true leadership are laid aside in the shuffle for power.

What can a structure do to prevent such failings? Basically, it cannot do anything. That is the nature of the beast and the only way it can be handled is to be killed. Here is a drastic proposal.

Every religious organization should have in its first constitution the irrevocable provision that it be disbanded and dispersed at the end of fifty years. For some, this limit should be twenty-five years. This would free the constituency to be more constantly in touch with God, thereby increasing openness for revival. It would free the organization from seeking wealth and prominence. Its funds would be channeled toward people. The non-Jesuslike structures would die and the church would not be as guilty of damaging people.

Such an approach would simply be recognizing the manner in which the Holy Spirit works, anyway. He keeps raising new movements that are alive and in touch with him, while the older structures get huffy and kick the new movement out. The new movement shows its vitality by growing faster than anything around until it may even become as big as the group from which it was expelled. Then the new group becomes rigid like the former one and another new movement, more in touch with the Holy Spirit and people, emerges and it in turn gets expelled by the new group that was expelled by the first one and on and on and on. Why not just move with the Holy Spirit and guarantee our death so we can multiply like a grain of wheat?

The humility of Jesus requires us to be gut-level honest about ourselves; yet systems that seek to preserve themselves tell only enough of the truth in their promotional material to encourage people to continue supporting them. Some promotional material makes a system sound alive and well long after it has died and decayed. To follow the style of Jesus is to refuse the temptation of self-promotion and glorification. It would mean accepting only the support of those who have volunteered their resources because they are grateful for service to them. The moment a structure begins to promote itself, it has violated the nature of Christ and has drunk the poison of its death.

Religious organizations should limit the amount of funds they hold in reserve. The more funds in reserve, the less we have to rely upon the Holy Spirit and the less we have to stay in servanthood to people. Even denominations should not lay up treasure where rust corrupts and thieves break in and steal. The Christ-nature isn't designed to horde large sums of money. Any time you see an organization with massive sums, you can count on scandal being uncovered at some point.

No system should violate the nature of Jesus by demanding anything of its people for the system's benefit. The kingdom of God is made up of volunteers. One who operates as a slave, a child, and the least can hardly be demanding toward others. Systems that do so are desperate and dying.

Every system should have as its first priority the building of relationships that will fulfill the command to love. No structure should be built that demands authority and obedience over love and unity. No person in the structure should be more than one step away in authority and contact from the constituency. No power should be granted simply on the basis of position. All authority must reside in the persons chosen of God and unless their lives and abilities have already granted them recognition, then no position should decree it. Institutional authority can never be a satisfactory replacement for God-given abilities and the authority which accompanies such gifts.

We must free ourselves from cultural forms such as elections (also called divisions of the house) and learn to make decisions that come out of unity produced by open and caring relationships — decisions from leaders who have renounced empire building — decisions carefully designed to violate no one.

We must free ourselves from viewing the clergy as an elite corps with privileges that come from ordination. Most such structures are merely preachers' unions that have little correlation to being servants.

When William Stringfellow declared all worldly institutions to be demonic because they do to people the same things demons do, he was close to the truth. I find it difficult to refute his statement.

Jesus walked among the people. He never became a part of any of the religious structures of his day except in areas such as the synagogue where the people were and where the lowest part of the pyramid of power lay. This fact should be a strong guideline for the religious world.

When we examine the life of Jesus, we discover that his anger was most kindled by those nestled within self-serving institutions who had lost sight of the needs of people and had long since ceased to be servants. Even the great commands of the past, such as "Remember the Sabbath day," had become institutional policies. Jesus put them back into perspective: "The Sabbath was made for man, not man for the Sabbath" (Mark 2:27).

All of Christ's love was aimed toward the redemption of man, not in an attempt to pigeonhole human actions and life, but to let mankind know the truth and be free. The law had to be subservient to love. Jesus got angry at any person or system that degraded or ignored people and their needs:

> "Woe to you, teachers of the law and Pharisees, you hypocrites! You give a tenth of your spices — mint, dill and cummin. But you have neglected the more important matters of the law — justice, mercy and faithfulness.
> You snakes! You brood of vipers! How will you escape being condemned to hell? Therefore I am sending you prophets and wise men and teachers. Some of them you will kill and crucify; others you will flog in your synagogues and pursue from town to town."
> (Excerpts from Matthew 23)

Apparently the Pharisees were so brainwashed by the system they had built that they now knew only how to destroy people with it. We must not be so blind as to think that those words of denunciation by Christ were only for a remote people. They are for today.

Somehow, God must erase centuries of misunderstanding in our minds and help us to see that the institutions and structures of the world and management systems that accompany them bear no relationship to the organic body of Christ. However efficient the world system, it cannot be automatically applied to the church.

One more Scripture that I wish to include speaks to our understanding of how Jesus lived in relation to the world-system (religious and secular) of his day. I leave it to you and the Holy Spirit to apply:

> The high priest carries the blood of animals into the Most Holy Place as a sin offering, but the bodies are burned outside the camp. And so Jesus also suffered outside the city gate to make the people holy through his own blood. Let us, then, go to him outside the camp, bearing the disgrace he bore. For here we do not have an enduring city, but we are looking for the city that is to come. (Hebrews 13:11-14)

Binding Us Together

If there is one thing that all the Christian world agrees about, it is that Jesus is Lord. Doctrinal fringes, cultural differences and individual ambitions have separated us into the splintered group that we are today. If there is to be the unity that Jesus prayed for, it will come around him and him alone.

At a gathering of Catholic sisters, I was one of a small number of Protestant ministers that was asked to address the group on the prospects for ecumenicism and on what we saw as separating us. The convolutions of church history and tradition were discussed with such knowledge and eloquence that I began to be embarrassed by the simplicity of my approaching statement. At my moment, I said, "I am a member of a very young denomination that has, nonetheless, developed many traditions of its own that would separate us. I do not want to tell you of them and you do not want to hear of them. You are members of a very old group with many more traditions than either of us wish to delve into today. Change in these patterns will not bring resolution and put us together. However, any time you want to get together and talk about Jesus, I am ready!" With that, I sat down. At the close, I was inundated by requests to come to their schools and say the same thing.

A few years ago I attended a conference in Singapore whose goal was to explore prospects for church unity and hear what God was saying to each other. Four hundred people from forty different denominations attended. After a week of intense interaction, the one statement to which all names could be freely signed was, "Jesus Christ is Lord!"

There may never be an organic world church and, were there one, it might be more an object of fear than of reverence. But living unity is coming because the Father answers the prayers of Jesus: "Holy Father, protect them by the power of your name — the name you gave me — so that they may be one as we are one . . . May they be brought to complete unity to let the world know that you sent me and have loved them even as you have loved me" (John 17:11, 23).

I have had the chance to see a good measure of church unity. It is always present when people are living the servant-style of Jesus. I have had a chance to see a good many church splits and it has become obvious that no church has ever split because two factions were arguing over who would get to be slave, or who would get to be least, or who would get to be last, or who would get to be of no reputation, or who would be the last to use force!

Unity comes out of our loving one another just as Jesus loves us. That is why we are given a description of his nature, so we will know how he loved us, how we can love one another and how the church can be unified.

At Home with the Body

If you are ready to begin the servant lifestyle, I would like to offer a place to get started and a direction to go. The recommendations here are certainly not the exclusive directions, however the fulfillment of servanthood demands an intimacy unfamiliar to many; so I share the experience of small groups with you so you can begin your own journey.

The early church discovered homes to be ideal places for the dynamics of Christianity to take place. There was no room for ritualistic trappings. The size made total participation possible and normative. Everyone would know each other so maintaining good relationships was of primary importance. Time would be available for prayer and ministering to each person. Scripture could be learned in dialogue and with immediate application.

Jesus himself chose twelve as his primary ministry

group. The nature of Jesus was one of love which demands close interpersonal relationships. Servanthood is difficult in large impersonal groupings. I have found that small groups can be successful when the nature of Jesus is used as a guiding force.

A leader who seeks to be a servant in a small group would control his own participation in order to free others. He would be sensitive to the needs expressed in order to minister to them. For example, he would not expect the other members of a group to share to any depth or answer any question that he had not shared or answered first. He would lead the way in listening and in affirming and in expressing his feelings honestly.

Out of humility he would indeed share his true feelings and lovingly confront when necessary. As a child he would accept persons at face value and would not probe into their lives, but would rejoice and weep with them. As one of no reputation, he would be willing to let the group see his own failings and struggles honestly.

As the younger he would be sensitive to when anyone was abusing someone else and would tend to protect them.

In all my studies and participation in small groups I have yet to see a proper leadership action that was not covered by the nature of Jesus. I consider it the secret of church life in small relational settings. The next three sections of this chapter discuss the techniques of helping those relationships grow.

Sharing Our Selves

"Fifth amendment, right to privacy" thinking has turned the body of Christ into a group of private individuals who meet together but remain in protective shells. In order to break out of this we must consciously share our selves with others. In spite of what you can know by observation, you can truly know me only when I relate my story with its struggles and feelings. To share my story, to deposit myself in vulnerability to others, is certainly in the order of servanthood.

Walking in the Sunshine

If you were involved in a group not built around the principles of the body, your self-revelation might well be followed by confrontation or a form of verbal attack/catharsis. But such are not the ways of the body. The body's response to a threatened or anxious member is protection. Our response to the self-revealer is affirmation.

The whole structure and process of the body of Christ is captured in a single statement of Paul in 1 Corinthians 12:7 as he declares that the gifts of the Spirit are given to *each one*, for edification or "building up," for the common good.

Paul's strongest statement about how we should view and respond to each other comes in 2 Corinthians 5:16-17: "So from now on we regard no one from a worldly point of view. Though we once regarded Christ in this way, we do so no longer. Therefore, if anyone is in Christ, he is a new creation; the old has gone, the new has come!"

In other words, I must now see you as the new creature you are. I must be able to discern the best. No longer can I say, "You're a good person, but . . ." and then launch into a diatribe about your faults. Your position as a child of God must be affirmed by me.

Sometimes I hear a protest to such affirmation and it usually takes this form: "But how are people going to know how to improve if I don't tell them what is wrong with them?" The answer is simple; Jesus states that our hearts already condemn us, so he didn't come to condemn but to offer abundant life.

If I were to ask you to write on a sheet of paper five things you don't like about yourself, you would likely be finished within sixty seconds. Then if I asked you to reverse the paper and write five things you like about yourself, you may need hours. We are painfully aware of our inadequacies.

A fairy tale (many of them seem near inspiration) expresses it well: The Sun and the North Wind observed a man walking along wearing a heavy overcoat. They decided to see who could get the coat off of him. The North Wind elected to try first. He blew a howling gale around him, but the stronger the wind the more tightly the man drew his coat around himself. Then the Sun said, "Now it's my turn." So, he beamed warming rays down upon the man, and soon, of his own choice, the man removed the coat and walked happily in the sunshine.

When we surround people with warmth, they will, by their own choice and energy, reveal and remove unnecessary heavy weights they have used as protection.

By sharing our histories with each other, we have deposited the most valuable thing we have — our revealed selves — with each other. Now that we have responded to that deposit with affirmation, a remarkable development occurs. We realize that our deposit is safe and we can risk even further; we can now trust.

The Freedom of Commitment

Armed with this new trust, we now are free to risk the commitment that before would have been too painful and, perhaps, even unproductive.

The first freedom of our new commitment is confession. James 5:16 proclaims: "Therefore confess your sins to each other and pray for each other so that you may be healed." Without trust, I will confess *your* sins or else confess socially acceptable and common sins such as "not enough faith or prayer." But with trust, I can share those things that truly hinder me and consequently, I can expect prayer and healing. Confession is like the daily elimination processes of the body. With confession, we can walk in comfort without unnecessary waste products. Infrequent confession creates a waste buildup that is traumatic indeed to eliminate.

Such confession also creates an appropriate form of discipline. By confession, I authorize others to pray for me and, also, to check back with me later to see how I am doing. Such gentle, regular accountability is woefully lacking in the church. As a result, we are pathologically independent and infected.

Our second freedom is to approach the Word of God personally through applicational Bible study. Applicational Bible study is basically confessional since it responds to two personal questions: What does the Bible say to me, and what am I going to do about it? The answers to these questions are confessions of our conviction by the Holy Spirit. Jesus and James call us clearly to such application: "Therefore everyone who hears these words of mine and puts them into practice is like a wise man who built his house on the rock" (Matthew 7:24). "Do not merely listen to the word, and so deceive yourselves. Do what it says" (James 1:22).

The third freedom of our commitment is confrontation. We seldom wait until after the process of trust building to confront areas in our relationship with each other that damage that relationship. When we do not wait, however, we cannot enjoy good fruit. With the process that builds trust, we have earned the right and the necessity to confront. For a reminder of the context of confrontation, reread the sections on humility and manipulation.

The fourth freedom of commitment is to the intimacy that the New Testament calls *koinonia*. We are no longer merely passengers together on the bus we call church, but we are desperately, eternally and intimately loyal to each other. Our dreams and visions as well as our goods become one another's property. We "forsake not the assembling of ourselves together."

At this stage we find completion of our servanthood. The love that servanthood expresses gives and receives in the constant, often unconscious, interaction of body life.

In the small group setting we discover that the body of Christ, like our own body, changes slowly and gently — but surely, even under such radical calls as issued in this book. If you are working with an old wineskin, the tenderizing process, if successful, must be slow and careful. At any rate, it is the wine that is important and must be preserved.

Sharing the Pain

A group of pastors with whom I had shared the principles of servanthood and who had been progressing in living them asked me to return for a weekend of retreat and discussion. One of them opened the weekend with this question, "Do you know how much pain you have caused us?" I admitted that I didn't know, apologized for causing their pain and urged them to return to their former ways. They replied, "Never!"

Their pains had begun to shift away from the frustrations of self-seeking to the empathetic pain of walking with others. Though that pain was greater, they never wanted to return to what they were before. Much suffering that is common to all is simply the product of our fallen human state — accidental injuries, sickness, disappointment. But such suffering is not necessarily the kind that is redemptive.

Paul states in Philippians 3:10, "I want to know Christ and the power of his resurrection and the fellowship of sharing in his sufferings. . . ." I am far more acquainted with the desire to know the power of his resurrection. Hebrews 5:8 tells us that Jesus learned obedience by what he suffered. All of the Scriptures that I have found indicate that the sufferings of Jesus were in *our* behalf and, were it not for *our behalf*, he would likely have had none but common sufferings.

Since Jesus said we would be treated as he was, it is logical that a practical outworking of following Jesus would be suffering in behalf of others.

One Word Follows Another

Once we grasp the all-encompassing servant nature of Jesus and begin to view all things through that lens, remarkable clarity comes to areas of the Scriptures that might have been murky before. Therefore, I here propose a new system of biblical interpretation that is both profound and simple.

If we agree that there is a basic internal agreement throughout the Bible, then we would have to go a step higher and agree that the written Word will not be contrary — ever — to the living Word — Jesus. True internal consistency of the Bible means that it is amenable to the nature of Jesus who was the complete revelation of God.

Consequently, no interpretation of any Scripture must place it at variance with his nature which was that of being slave, example, humble, child, younger, last, least, no reputation, no force, etc. Any

Scripture whose interpretation on our part is at variance with the nature of Jesus must be set aside until we have enough light to interpret it properly. It remains as Scripture. Yet we admit that because the way we presently view it is not consistent with the nature of Jesus, we do not understand it well enough to proclaim it.

By now, you can recognize that some Scripture which is currently used for doctrine and lifestyle is in trouble if we try to harmonize it with the nature of Jesus. That should simply let us know that we have interpreted it wrongly.

It is important, too, that we not fall prey to thinking that the Bible is the fourth member of the Godhead. The Bible is the written revelation of God, but regardless of what we believe about it, it must never violate the One it was written to reveal.

The Style for All Seasons

The revivals of this century have primarily been Pentecostal or charismatic in nature. The rediscovery of the gifts of the Spirit by the Pentecostals and their outstanding fervor prompted them to believe and teach that their revival was *the* end-time revival. They felt that there was nothing left to rediscover in Scripture, thus their charismatic phenomena represented the ultimate — the revival of revivals.

Though the Pentecostals did restore to the church a neglected, even lost, power principle, they have not swept the church and world with the unity and effectiveness that one would expect of ultimacy. Despite their Jesus-centered worship and enthusiasm, the major emphasis for which they became known was not this knowledge of Jesus but instead their consortium with the Holy Spirit. It is the glossolalic emphasis that is immediately apparent rather than the christological, although, for both the Pentecostals and Charismatics, the strength of their relationship to Christ is unquestionable.

Perhaps the grand scheme is unfolding, that the Holy Spirit, now having achieved the attention of a broader spectrum of the church and world, is preparing to sweep aside mythological entanglements and the Jesus of nostalgia and fulfill his major predicted function — that of glorifying Christ.

In the Gospel of John, Jesus foretold the coming and the action of the Holy Spirit:

> "The Holy Spirit . . . will teach you all things
> and will remind you of everything I have
> said to you."
> "When the Counselor comes, whom I will
> send to you . . . he will testify about me."
> "He will guide you into all truth."
> "He will bring glory to me by taking from
> what is mine and making it known to you."
> (John 14:26; 15:26; 16:13; 16:14)

The most apparent conclusion to be drawn is that the Holy Spirit, as his primary function, will reveal the nature of Jesus to us and convict the world about him. The revivals of emphasis on the Holy Spirit violated this very principle by focusing on the Holy Spirit rather than letting the Spirit speak to us and the world about the person of Jesus.

I believe the world's final great revival will be a revival that centers on Jesus himself and his nature.

The world has seen no power greater than that of Jesus, and the church exercises no power greater than that of living the loving lifestyle of Jesus.

We cannot escape the call and command given by Jesus to his church: "Peace be with you! As the Father has sent me, I am sending you" (John 20:21).

Can we honestly believe that we are to be sent *partially* as the Father sent Jesus? Surely not. We must accept that we are sent with the same nature, the same requirements of attitude that were given to Jesus.

The work of the gifts to the body of Christ is to equip us to minister to each other in a way that will bring us into a likeness of Christ: "Until we all reach unity in the faith and in the knowledge of the Son of God and become mature, attaining to the whole measure of the fullness of Christ" (Ephesians 4:13).

Our maturity is to make us like Christ. Our ministry is to mature others to be like Christ. To be like Christ we must have his mind and absorb his nature.

If the things spoken about the nature of Christ in this book are true, then the Holy Spirit will quicken them to you and help you apply them in your own unique way. The implications listed in prior chapters are things that the Holy Spirit has dealt with me about in my own life. They need not be your quickenings. Whether those implications are confirmed in your mind or not, you still must respond somehow to the call to be like Jesus, taste of his power, fellowship in his sufferings and become like him in his death.

Lest you end this book feeling a load of guilt and hopelessness about whether you will ever attain to the maturity and fullness of him, I wish to share an encouraging word from Scripture:

> For it is God who works in you to will and to act according to his good purpose. (Philippians 2:13)
> For we are God's workmanship, created in Christ Jesus to do good works, which God prepared in advance for us to do. (Ephesians 2:10)

I worked in an office once where the men of the office would take lunch hours on Tuesdays and Thursdays to play basketball in a gymnasium across the street. Now, basketball is not my best game. When we would choose up sides, it threatened to go this way: "Gentlemen, we had Gayle last time. It's your turn to take him. . . ."

So, you can see that I was mainly there for the exercise. However, there was one fellow named Dave who was six feet eighteen inches tall when he stepped onto the basketball court. I loved to get on his team. We would always win. All I had to do was get the ball to Dave and he would score. When we would get the ball back, I would dribble it around a while simply for appearance sake, lob the ball over to Dave and he would dunk it for another two points. Then I would say, "Aren't we good?"

That is much like the relationship we have with Jesus. He is the one who is at work in us to help us want to do his will and then to help even more as we try to do it. We are his workmanship. What we are is his full responsibility and he accepts it. Our job is to stay on the same team as he, cast our cares on him, and let him do the scoring against Satan for us: "The one who is in you is greater than the one who is in the world" (1 John 4:4).

So make yourself available to him. Permit his Holy Spirit to make you aware of the mind of Christ as it works its way out in your life. Give yourself away and keep growing!

Let us fix our eyes on Jesus, the author and perfecter of our faith, who for the joy set before him endured the cross, scorning its shame, and sat down at the right hand of the throne of God. (Hebrews 12:2)

STUDY GUIDE

The main theme of *The Jesus Style* is that Jesus is the full revelation of the Father and that the clearest definition of his nature is found in the "Greatest in the Kingdom" teachings of Jesus and other passages that surround that theme. The primary trait that flows through the book is "servanthood." The theme is further condensed to being "others-centered," and much of the content with its applications can be better understood if that hyphenated word is understood or kept in consciousness.

Written in short, unnumbered chapters, *The Jesus Style* is ideal for group study or personal devotion. If used with a group, some advance preparation is suggested for the leader. To keep the overall theme in front of you as you go through each set of questions, copy the list of fourteen traits found in the questions in this study guide under *"The Jesus Style—Within Our Reach"* and give each student a copy or make a poster listing them to place in your study area.

Although there are some information-gathering times in this study guide, most questions are applicational in nature and ideally suited for small group study.

A Style of His Own —Jesus, Yes

1. John the Baptist and the apostles of Jesus seemed to be locked into typical cultural thinking. From what you have read in the book and from your awareness of other scriptures, what events in the New Testament seem to indicate to you that people expected Jesus to fit into a certain style of life or teaching?

2. If Jesus were to come today for the first time, what things would he need to do to be made most acceptable to you and to others? How do you think he would dress today? What country do you think would be most responsive to his teaching? Why? Which country do you think would most quickly try to stop his work?

3. The culture of the Kingdom and the cultures of the world seem to be in constant conflict. To help you understand how easily this occurs, think of any people who have come to your neighborhood from a foreign country. How different are they? What adjustments have they had to make in food, clothing, language and customs? If you have ever visited a foreign country, how much adjustment did you have to make? In what ways were you comfortable and uncomfortable?

The Jesus Approach

1. Think carefully about the following list from this chapter and mark each one that you think would cause you or others to be very cautious before following a person thus described:

Born in a Barn
Born in an Insignificant Village
Birth of Questionable Legitimacy
Some Highly Embarrassing Ancestors
Only the Lowest Class People Invited to Celebrate His Birth
He Was Not Handsome
He Grew Up in a Bad Neighborhood
He Was Poor and Seemed Content to Be
His Advance-Man Was Abrasive and Somewhat Strange
His Closest Followers Were Inept and Argumentative
The Government Placed Him on Shameful Death Row

2. Which item or items above do you think would cause a candidate for public office to resign from the race if the press publicized it?

3. We learn from this chapter that Jesus was "nonthreatening or nonmanipulative" in order to free us to make a genuine decision about him. Jot down in your notebook some of the people or forces that influence your decisions and put a + sign beside the ones you are most "anxious" about. When do you feel you have made the most "honest" decisions—the ones that truly came from your heart and desires?

4. Jot down a description of your spiritual heritage. What influence does this have on your decisions? What areas of spiritual adventure have you declined to pursue because of this heritage? How has your heritage drawn you into spiritual adventure?

The Style Setter — Number One

1. This book and especially this chapter strongly maintains that Jesus was everything that God is and that he is the full and final revelation of God. Make two lists side-by-side in your notebook. On one side, list the things that you feel you know about Jesus and on the other list those ways you feel you have really experienced him.

2. Read Colossians 1:15–2:10. Notice the number of times Paul uses the word "all" and other superlatives. In what areas of your life would you like to use the word "all" about Jesus?

3. With the set of the traits of Jesus (You prepared it in the first set of questions) in front of you, read Colossians 2:8 aloud and list any "traditions or philosophies" that you think do not fit the nature or principles of Christ.

4. Often, people find it uncomfortable to simply talk about Jesus. Do you find this to be so? With which friends do you think you could break that barrier and carry on a conversation about Jesus?

5. What "successful" ministries trouble you because some things about them do not seem to fit the nature of Jesus? Pause now and pray for them.

The Style Setter — One for All

1. This chapter makes some strong statements about the necessity to love one another as indicated in John 13:34, 35. What are the ways you have normally been able to tell that someone was a Christian? How do those measuring systems compare to this command?

2. Jesus said to love one another "as I have loved you." With the set of traits of Jesus in front of you (from the first set of questions) meditate on each trait with the thought that this is the way Jesus is toward you. How does this fit with your definition of love?

3. Who are some of the people you feel display those (or some of them) "servant" traits toward you? How do you try to do that for others?

The Style Setter—All for One

1. This chapter makes more strong statements about love, claiming on the basis of Matthew 22:40 that loving God and your neighbor is what the Bible is all about. Are you content that this is so or does it trouble you in some way? If it troubles you, express why or jot it in your notebook.

2. Read whatever creeds you can find and, if it is readily available to you, read the statement of beliefs of your own church organization. What references to love among the followers of Jesus do you find? Is loving each other a criterion for being a member of your church? How would you go about knowing if someone was a loving person?

3. This chapter contains two lists about love. Write down each list on separate sheets of paper. If you are in a group, give each member a copy of each sheet. Now, with these two lists plus the constant list of the traits of Jesus that you keep, read them all aloud—in unison if you are in a group—then share the thoughts that came to your mind as you read them. How can one list be a tool to help you fulfill the other?

4. You can have a fascinating and inspiring time by taking the three lists from the question above and using them as guidelines to write a creed or a set of theological beliefs as if you were a "founding father" of a spiritual institution.

The Style Setter—One of Many

1. This chapter is constructed around the great "high priest" prayer of Jesus in John 17. Parts of this remarkable prayer are rather disturbing in the light of our observable church situation, specifically "that we may be one." In what ways are you seeing this prayer fulfilled? How does it seem unfulfilled to you? Pause and pray for those "unfulfilled" situations.

2. In these same chapters that Jesus talked about love (John 13–17) he also spoke of fruit. If fruit is our love and the result of it, what fruit of our lives might be the most observable by our neighbors? By our fellow church members?

3. Jesus attaches successful evangelism to our "being one" or loving one another. Between meetings, have each member

of your group ask ten people how they became a Christian. Compare notes and see how many of them were "convinced" and how many of them were won by someone who "loved" them. Tell your own story in your notebook or to your group of how you became a follower of Jesus.

4. Now that you have three lists of loving traits and fruit, make a list of the ones in which you specifically need strength and ask someone to pray for you about them.

The Jesus Style—Within Our Reach

1. This chapter turns our minds back to the chapter called *The Jesus Approach.* Since that list of the ways Jesus revealed himself cannot likely be ours personally, share the things in your life that would be "your list"—those things that make you approachable, vulnerable to others.

2. The scriptures written in this chapter begin the introduction to the list of the traits of Jesus that you have been using since the beginning of the book. Read the scriptures aloud or in unison, taking note of the unifying threads contained in them.

3. Following is the list of the traits of Jesus. They are the most important bits of knowledge in the book, yet they are not listed as a unit within the book. Copy these down and memorize them—they will serve you well. They are also needed for your use in other question sets. The first eight traits come from the Gospels and the last six from Philippians which will be discussed later, but the whole list is presented here for your use:

Servant
Not lord it over others
Example
Humble
As a child
As the younger
As the least
As the last
Used no force
Was not driven by blind ambition
Made himself of no reputation
Completely human

Obedient
Gave up his life

4. In the John 13–17 teachings, Jesus had much to say about the role of the Holy Spirit in speaking about Jesus. What experiences have you had with the Holy Spirit and how did they affect your knowledge of and view of Jesus?

The Jesus Style—At Your Service

1. This chapter begins the core of the book and establishes the first trait of the nature of Jesus—servanthood. Another word for servanthood might be "others-centered." What does the word "servant" normally bring to your mind?

2. Who are the persons who make life better for you? For whom do you make life better?

3. If you fully realized your ambitions, what tension would it create in terms of the call to servanthood?

4. The author states that servanthood is a choice we make and is not the result of coercion. Then he spends most of the chapter on the problems created by manipulation. For one who is others-centered, being the object of manipulation hangs as a constant danger. Think of some ways you feel others have taken advantage of you. How do you feel and react when this happens to you?

5. You may have noticed that you try to avoid a person who attempts to manipulate you. If a person successfully takes advantage of you, you may notice that you dislike him or her for so doing and yourself for being trapped. Here are some statements that might be useful to you in avoiding manipulation:

"I am uncomfortable with the choice I have to make here so I am going to have to say 'no.'"

"Under the circumstances, I don't feel I have the ability to make a loving choice, so I must say 'no.'"

"I am doing this because I choose to. I think it is right and best."

6. Ask a friend or members of your group to role-play a manipulative situation with you and practice using the statements above until you are comfortable with them.

7. Servanthood and servitude are not the same thing. Servanthood is the result of choice and servitude is the result of force. Using "servanthood" and "servitude" as the heading of two columns, take the following verses and jot down the parts that fit under each column: John 10:17, 18; 1 Corinthians 9:19; Matthew 5:38–42.

8. What are the needs or forces that truly "drive" you? Discuss them with someone and describe where your ability to "choose" can be used.

The Jesus Style—The Power Pyramid

1. This chapter establishes the second trait in the nature of Jesus—not lording it over others. Few actions in life are clearer than man's drive to have power over others. Action from this drive fills the pages of our newspapers. Take the current copy of your local newspaper and see how many articles have been generated by an individual or group trying to exercise some power over others.

2. This chapter tells us that those who lord it over others do so at the sacrifice of honesty from their subordinates. To test this, list some businessmen, politicians or religious leaders whom you know. Think of things being said about them that you don't believe they know about. How comfortable would you be telling them? Pray about your role as an honest person in their lives.

3. How has submission to spiritual authority in your life brought growth to you? In what ways have you seen spiritual authority abused?

4. Much of this chapter applies the nature of Jesus to marriage and family. If you see your children as God's children whom you are caring for, what things would you want them to know about God, their Father, and what would you want to tell them about your own responsibility? How would you interpret "equipping" your children from Ephesians 4:12? List the most important things, in order, that you want your children to have or know.

5. If you are a husband, with the traits of Jesus list in front of you, jot down in your notebook some ways this list could apply

to "loving your wife as Jesus loved the Church." If you are a wife, jot down some ways you feel you submit yourself to the Lord and note how that can apply to your relationship to your husband.

6. What are some things you do that promote your "coupleness," thus your mutual submission? How do those "coupleness" actions compare in number to your attempts to express your individuality?

7. What systems of strong authority have you observed around you?

8. Whom do you tend to "listen to" and how would you describe their authority over you?

9. When you are in charge, how would you describe how you perform?

The Jesus Style—I'd Rather See a Sermon

1. This chapter develops the third trait in the nature of Jesus—example. Go back to your childhood years and think of some people who "showed you how" to do things. Describe how you felt when you learned new skills. To whom are you a "show-you-how" person?

2. A pastor once preached a sermon on "Some Things I Am Sick and Tired Of." His points went this way: "I am sick and tired of expecting you to pray when I have not been praying. I am sick and tired of expecting you to give when I have not been giving. I am sick and tired of expecting you to witness when I have not been witnessing." Isn't that refreshing to hear? What "spiritual skills" do you feel you have and who "showed you how"? What spiritual skills would you like for someone to teach you?

3. This chapter makes some strong statements about education and educational systems. How do you feel about education as you know it? Education truly makes a student like his teacher. How do you go about choosing a teacher for your children? Do you know of any place that chooses teachers primarily because their lives are worth copying? If you were (or are) a teacher, how much would you want your students to know about your life?

194

4. In Deuteronomy 6:6, 7 God tells the Israelis to teach their children the commands he gives them *today*. What is God saying to you *today*? Does anyone else, especially your children, know about it? Jot down in your notebook or share with your group some things God is saying to you *today*.

5. With the list of the traits of Jesus in front of you, see if you can devise an educational system that would copy Jesus closely and cause those traits to come about in students' lives.

6. Describe some things you have learned that you feel could only be learned by observation.

7. What things have you learned merely by hearing or reading about them?

8. How much have you learned spiritually by seeing examples you don't want to follow and how much by seeing the proper example?

9. In what area of growth are you now struggling where you need a good example to follow?

10. Who are the people whose lives might be affected by your example?

11. What do you think is the strongest areas in which you can teach by example?

The Jesus Style—No More, No Less

1. This chapter declares the fourth trait in the nature of Jesus—humility. What comes to your mind when you hear the word "humble"?

2. Humility can be described as an "honesty and openness" principle. It would be difficult to do much teaching by example (as discussed in the prior chapter) without humility or the willingness to be honestly seen by others. What is the image you try to uphold to others? What are the ways you go about upholding that image? How expensive and time-consuming is it? How accurate is the image you want to portray?

3. The right to privacy is constitutionally guaranteed in the United States. That is great for our society but has some real pitfalls in the body of Christ. What things about yourself do you

not want your Christian friends to know? Take some time now to confess these to the Lord and, if you can, share them with a trusted friend so that friend can pray for you.

4. Second Corinthians 3:17, 18 contains a little-noticed but powerful principle—that of keeping ourselves revealed to God—which then causes God to shine his glory upon us and change us into his likeness. Write in your notebook and share with your group some areas that you have confessed to God which have now changed for the better in your life.

5. If your feelings (not thoughts) were projected on a screen, how surprised do you think people would be? What feelings do you think would surprise them most?

6. When, especially during church times, do you find your feelings different from what others seem to have? How would you feel if you had to reveal the difference?

7. Whatever fears of self-disclosure you have, list them and boldly ask the Lord to express his grace to you and remove the fears.

The Jesus Style—A Child Is . . .

1. This chapter develops the fifth trait in the nature of Jesus—being as a child. Spend some time adventuring in your childhood; remember your games, your friends, your Christmases, your fun. How can you remember your faith developing as a child? Adventure further by playing an old childhood game with your group—pick-up-sticks, marbles, jacks, etc. Observe your own feelings and the laughter of your group.

2. Spend some time with children to help you grow in Nature-of-Jesus skills. If you can, practice getting on the floor with them. Give them space or they may be frightened, but they will quickly feel comfortable around you. When you see a child being held by its mother, practice catching the child's eyes and trying to make the child smile.

3. Being unthreatening grates against our nature. We would rather be known as strong—the "don't tread on me" feeling. How would the political power of the church in the U.S.A. compare with some other countries? Whose commitment and growth would you expect to be better, ours or theirs? Do you

respond differently (more honestly maybe?) to people of whom you are not afraid? Think of some people you might be intimidated by and describe how you tend to protect yourself from them.

4. A child is described as being unable to deceive. How do you feel around people you know are hiding something from you? What do you think would happen in the church if we were suddenly unable to hide anything?

5. When you read the Genesis story of Adam and Eve, you notice that the first thing they did after they sinned was to hide. Jesus, our new Adam, tells us that we are "a city set on a hill which cannot be hid," and "the light of the world." Discuss with your group or write in your notebook some things these statements can mean for you.

6. What do you consider to be positive and negative traits of a child?

7. Think of some commands that you hear adults give to you. How would these words sound to you if they were coming from a child?

8. Who tends to bring out the child or playful qualities in you and how do they do it?

The Jesus Style—The Hand-Me-Down Set

1. This chapter brings us to the sixth trait in the nature of Jesus—being as the younger. One of the best words to describe the position of "younger" as meant by Jesus would be "pilgrim." A pilgrim is one passing through; he has no stake in the world or its systems. Read Hebrews 11:8–10 and Hebrews 11:13–15 aloud. Now make two lists in your notebook: one list of those things one probably would do and not do if he were a pilgrim and another list of those things one would do or not do if he were a citizen or settler of a country. Now, the difficult question is, "Spiritually, on which one of these lists do I tend to fall?" Discuss this with your group or make another list of things from which you might want God to free you.

2. What is your birth position (first, second, third, etc.) in your family and how do you think it has affected you?

3. What privileges do you have that you would hate to give up?

4. How do you feel when you hear of groups protesting their "rights"? Would you protest to protect your own rights? Would you protest to protect the rights of other Christians? How aware are you of the freedoms of Christians in other lands? Discuss that with your group.

5. Have you ever packed too much for a journey and wished, as you were carrying the heavy load, that you had packed lighter? What things do you have that you feel are absolute minimum in order for you to live as a Christian? In your notebook write down all the things you can think of which the Early Church did not have but that we now have relative to church.

The Jesus Style—Bringing Up the Rear

1. This chapter brings us to the seventh item in the nature of Jesus—being last. Being last is the "last" thing we want to have happen to us. Since this doesn't mean to be last just to show how great we are, just what does it mean to you? What comes to your mind as ways to obey this statement of Jesus about being last? When do you usually try to be first?

2. What are some situations in which your being last has benefited others?

3. This chapter declares that competition within the body of Christ is unthinkable. How do you feel about that? What contests have you been in and how was the winner determined? How many losers were there in that contest? Do you consider yourself a winner or loser? If you think you are a winner, how do you feel about competition? If you feel you are a loser, how do you feel about competition?

4. Just for the fun of it, see if you can devise a contest in which the highest attributes are measured, such as love, faithfulness, servanthood.

5. The author does state that he believes competition can be redeemed in certain ways. See if you can invent a game that redeems competition.

6. Gayle Erwin has written a creed for Christian athletes and teams. React to it with your group or in your notebook. How different do you think church athletic leagues would be if they all followed this creed?

Athlete's Creed

I am a follower of Jesus Christ and a member of
His body above all other memberships.
In all activities I will seek to build and
strengthen the Body of Christ.
I will seek recreation that grows out of
fellowship and makes fellowship grow.
I will seek to follow kingdom principles in all areas
of sports and will esteem others better than myself.
I will operate in my recreational activities in such ways
that all my brothers will win regardless of the score.
I will play as if Jesus were both my teammate and opponent.

7. When risk is involved, being first is like being last. When have you been first to take a chance for the benefit of others?

The Jesus Style—Room in the Manger

1. The eighth trait in the nature of Jesus—being least—is discussed in this chapter. Our drive within the church for honor, recognition and praise prompts the author to use such strong words as "scandal" and "shamelessly compromised." How do you feel about recognition systems in the church? What do you think when you hear of someone being given an honorary degree?

2. The author states that "least" is not the cellar for the indolent and inadequate, but is the result of a loving choice. Is there anyone you are trying to put first because you love him or her and think it would do that person good? Think quietly and privately about those secret things you do to try to bless and honor someone.

3. Read aloud the song Mary sang in response to the announcement by the angel about the birth of Jesus (Luke 1:46–55). With that kind of understanding, what kinds of things do you think Mary might have taught Jesus as he was growing up?

The Jesus Style—Good-bye Strong Arm Tactics

1. The focus shifts from the Gospels to the letter by Paul to the Philippians and the great "mind of Christ" song in 2:5–11. Begin this section by reading aloud that passage. This chapter adds traits nine and ten to the list of his nature—using no force and not being driven by blind ambition.

2. Do you ever wish that Jesus would use all his power to simply stop all crime and wrongdoing? How would you feel if you were forced to do something you didn't want to do? Jesus chose not to use force on anyone. Usually, when someone feels he was forced to do something, he tends to try to sabotage the situation. Discuss some times when you have tried to show resistance to a "forced" situation.

3. Can you think of a time when you were truly given freedom to make a choice without having outside influence on you? Describe it.

4. When have you seen someone who was "down" exploited? How did you feel about it? Were you moved to do anything?

5. Evangelism is presented as an area filled with blind ambition. Often we use whatever tactics are at hand, godly or not, to win the lost because we need the statistics. This is an example of having a great "end" but using dubious "means." See if you can list some ways we can effectively witness using proper means. Jot down or discuss how many of them you can or will do.

6. What other questionable methods have you seen used to accomplish what appears to be a good ministry goal? What do you think would cause good people to use questionable means? Have you ever been taken advantage of by someone who was trying to achieve a good goal? How?

7. Satan tempted Jesus to try to gain the world by changing his focus from God to Satan, but Jesus stayed faithful. What would you consider to be your goals in life? How are you working to achieve them? How have you been tempted to use inappropriate methods to achieve your goals?

The Jesus Style—Hello, I'm Reverend . . .

1. The eleventh trait of the nature of Jesus packs a wallop—he made himself of no reputation or made himself nothing. I like to be seen with people who improve my image. I am an incurable name-dropper. Disturbingly, Jesus reveled in the presence of the unseemly. This, of course, was so the unseemly could revel in the presence of Jesus. Jesus was approachable to the lowest of persons—even the chained, demon-possessed. Who are some famous or powerful people you have met or been around? How intimidated did you feel in their presence? What could have changed that feeling of intimidation?

2. Whom do you have difficulty approaching now because of his or her reputation or fame?

3. Who would you consider to be the "lowest reputation" people in your town? How comfortable do you think they would be with you? Can you think of anything that might make them more at ease with you?

4. How do you think people see you? What do you do to help them see you that way? What title do you have or item do you own that you think might make others jealous?

5. Jesus also made himself nothing by becoming poor so we could be rich. How do you feel around people who are rich? Is it similar to being around the famous? If you are rich, how would people know it? If you are rich, what do you do to make the poor comfortable around you?

6. How much time do you spend taking care of what you own? Do you ever want to get away from it all? Why do you sometimes feel that way? What do you do when you get a "few extra dollars"?

7. How do you feel that the display of wealth by a church (such as an extravagant building) fits in with the nature of Jesus?

The Jesus Style—Down to Earth

1. It is truly difficult to think of Jesus as human; it seems to violate something in our minds to reduce him to our level, but

human he was and that is the twelfth item in our traits of Jesus. What are some normal "human" activities that you have never thought that Jesus would do? Do you suppose he ever needed to have his laundry done?

2. Think of some of your own temptations. In what ways can you imagine Jesus being tempted by the same thing?

3. How different do you think Jesus actually was from you? Why do you think that?

4. What does it mean to you to be "fully human"?

5. The author uses this chapter to talk about forgiveness under the title of "Living Without Weights." Why do you suppose it is here? What does it mean to you as a human being to "identify" with another person? How can recognizing your own humanity help us to forgive others?

6. Some interesting and inspiring studies have been made about the power of touch. The Bible reveals to us that Jesus went everywhere "touching" people—even the untouchables. What does touch mean to you and how does this relate to Jesus being human? If you feel like making another list, try finding and jotting down all the people in the New Testament whom Jesus touched.

The Jesus Style—Like Father, Like Son

1. The thirteenth trait of Jesus tells us that he was obedient. Jesus told us that he only said what he heard the Father say and only did what he saw the Father do. That means that this list of traits of Jesus was also a description of the Father and Jesus was obedient to that nature. Read Matthew 16:24, 25 aloud and discuss or write down what this means to you now that you have the traits of the nature of Jesus before you or in your memory. What does "come after me" now mean to you?

2. What do you think would happen in your life if you felt you were "anointed"? The anointing of the Holy Spirit that Jesus speaks of in Luke 4:18 apparently gave him the power to be obedient to the Father. How does the list of beneficiaries of his anointing compare to the list of the traits of Jesus?

3. On one side of your notebook page make a list of the actions resulting from the anointing. Beside each action place a

number from zero to ten to indicate how you feel you are doing in your own action toward those people. You may want to use several versions of the Bible and also to read Isaiah 61 to enlarge your list as much as you can (see the list below).

THE ANOINTING

Preach good news to the poor   0–10
Bind up the brokenhearted
Proclaim freedom for the captives
Release for the prisoners
Recovery of sight for the blind
Set at liberty them that are bruised
Release the oppressed
Proclaim the year of the Lord's favor

4. How would you express the Lord's favor to someone? In your opinion, why didn't Jesus say the anointing brought him to express the Lord's anger?

The Jesus Style —Shepherds Don't Run

1. Jesus paid the ultimate price of servanthood, his life, and that brings us to the fourteenth and final trait in our list—death. That thought brings rather evocative questions: What truly drives me? For what am I willing to die?

2. Many people have died in the past to achieve or guarantee certain privileges for us. Are there any who come to mind for whose deaths you are thankful?

3. What dreams of yours have died and been resurrected?

4. The death of Jesus was not simply death as a "natural" event but death as the result of his servanthood. Take some time to talk or write about that often taboo subject—your own physical death and preparations you are making for it. Now, take the time to write or share your reason for staying alive.

The Jesus Style —Serendipity

1. It would be reasonable to think that it was all over when Jesus died, but Philippians 2:9–11 hurls our souls aloft with a song of exultation. Read it aloud.

2. Obviously, the success of servanthood can only be brought about by God himself. Take some time to hunt other scriptures where humility and servanthood "pays off."

3. This passage evokes worship as we read it. Do another study, especially in Revelations, the last book of the New Testament, of worship passages like this one that seem to explode with joy and exultation.

4. How has God honored you for working secretly or behind the scenes or with a servant's heart?

The Jesus Style — The Power Broker

1. Jesus used the servant act of footwashing to teach us three major lessons:

    A. What to do to show complete love
    B. What we will do when we know who we are
    C. How to handle power so it won't corrupt

Since footwashing was the lowest job in the house, the first lesson brings a natural question: For whom are you willing to do the "dirty work"? What is the lowest job at your house? Who does it?

The second lesson prompts this question: If someone asked you just who you are, what would you say? How did you come to believe these things about yourself? In what way do you think you could "lose face"? Do you suppose the disciples thought Jesus "lost face" by washing their feet? If not, why?

You have heard the statement: Power corrupts and absolute power corrupts absolutely. To respond to lesson three, list the ways you have power. Keep in mind that such things as your money, skin color, passport are power symbols. In what ways are you using these forms of power to "wash feet"? Discuss this statement: The only way to use power so that it does not corrupt you and damage others is by servant-hearted, others-centered actions.

2. The seating arrangement at the Last Supper was by rank (which may have been the reason the apostles argued so frequently). What "seating by rank" do you experience now and how does it affect you? Do you ever get to sit at the "head

table"? Would you question whether some of the people seated at the "head table" really deserve to be there?

  3. Discuss or write about your own ambitions at this time.

Living in Style—The Sweet and the Bitter

  1. How do you feel about this study in the Nature of Jesus so far? How comfortable or uncomfortable have the questions been for you?

  2. Are you finding the message to be enjoyable but the living out of the message to be more difficult? Which areas are you finding most difficult at this time?

  3. Is it possible that this lifestyle is impossible? Why do you think it is or isn't?

Living in Style—The Ankle Bone
Connected to the Foot Bone

  1. The author believes that the only way the "body" of Christ can succeed, even live, is when each part becomes a servant to the rest of the body. In what ways do you see that concept working or not working in your experience?

  2. Several humorous illustrations are used in this chapter to show how ridiculous certain church actions would be if the parts of the human body operated that way. See if you can come up with some more illustrations in that vein.

  3. If cancer is a selfish cell that serves only itself and grows at the expense of the body, how can you use that understanding to be discerning about actions in the body of Christ? Can you recognize which actions in your circle of experience might be cancerous now?

  4. How much time does your body spend taking care of itself? How much time does your church body spend taking care of itself?

Living in Style—Prisoners of History

  1. This is one of the more controversial chapters in the book as the author claims that denominations and other religious

institutions tend to violate the traits of Jesus by their very nature. He feels that new movements organize themselves for benevolent reasons but then lapse into self-propagating and self-isolating behavior. How do you feel about this dilemma? What do you think is the role of denominations today? How has your denomination brought you closer to some and kept you away from others?

2. Do you think your denomination acts with a servant heart? How, if ever, have you tried to make it more servant-hearted? Did it work? If so, for how long?

3. The author proposes a preposterous idea of having all new organizations disband themselves after 25–50 years and give their assets to the poor. Since that action will not likely happen, what do you think can be done to preserve the fervor or a revival or new movement that seems typically to wane after a period of 25–50 years?

4. Have you ever found yourself more loyal to an organization than to Jesus or the body of Christ? How do you reconcile "exclusiveness" and the nature of Jesus?

Living in Style—Binding Us Together

1. You are reading an unusually "neutral" book in spite of our discoveries of the last chapter. From an organizational or denominational point of view, you cannot determine whose "side" the author is on. Instead, these studies have focused our minds on Jesus and our response to him, which is why the book has been so widely used by different groups. Now that you have experienced this, if you desire a truly creative spiritual experience, see if you can gather eight to twelve people of different denominational backgrounds and begin the study again.

2. Make a list of all the churches in your community and pray for a different one each day.

3. One of the unfortunate paradoxes of churches of any title is that many of them are in a state of internal conflict. In your group or from your memory, make another list of those churches that you know might be hurting from such conflict. With the list of the traits of Jesus in front of you to guide you, pray specifically for unity and healing for those churches.

206

4. Examine your own set of beliefs and see if there are segments that one "must" believe before you can fellowship with him. Do those segments have anything to do with Jesus himself? Now, are there any positions not on your list which if a person believes "that," you cannot fellowship with him? Does "that" unacceptable belief have anything to do with Jesus? If you wish to discuss these answers, do so, but especially pray about your stance.

5. Call some members or pastors of other churches and tell them you appreciate the work they are doing for God and you are praying that God will be very present with them and increase their ministry.

6. Think of some religious subjects that have caused "hot" discussions in your life. Were they about something other than Jesus himself? Next time you are in a religious discussion make this statement: "Let's talk about Jesus." Report to your group the outcome.

7. Walk around the block and pray for the occupants of each house you pass.

Living in Style — At Home with the Body

1. If the statements of Jesus in John 13:34, 35 about loving one another are to be believed, then relationships are a foundation stone of Christianity. How do you go about trying to build relationships? What would you do if you learned that a neighbor of yours was a new Christian?

2. In this chapter, the author makes a case for the use of smaller groupings for Bible study and fellowship. What experience have you had with small groups?

3. The author borrows Lyman Coleman's relationship-building progression in this chapter. These steps in succession are first to reveal ourselves to each other (tell our story, etc.), then affirm each other, then commit ourselves to each other. Who knows your life story or testimony? Take the time to hear someone else's story and to tell yours. This will take a few hours so give it enough time. If you are starting a new small group, take an hour or so each meeting to hear a person's story. Be sure to express afterward to the person who has told his story the ways you have seen Jesus in him.

4. The third stage of relationships—commitment—permits us to be even more open or confessional to one another. If you have come to this stage you will find that prayer is much more powerful and honest. Write down or share the names of those persons who know your true needs and are praying for you. Also list those persons whose needs you know and are praying for.

5. Experiment with Matthew 20:1-16 for an applicational Bible study. Brainstorm in your group or alone the answers to the following questions in order: 1. What does this passage reveal to me about God? 2. What does this passage reveal to me about myself? 3. What commands do I feel are here for me to follow? Your relationship with your group will determine the degree of depth you will reach in your study.

6. In your private prayer, practice revealing yourself to God as indicated in 2 Corinthians 3:18. Tell God everything about your current feelings and desires. If you feel your prayers don't work, tell him that. If you feel powerless in conquering certain problems, tell him that. Don't leave anything unrevealed to him.

Living in Style—Sharing the Pain

1. Living for others will probably increase your pain. You now will notice the hurts of others more than before and that will make you acutely aware of the daily agony of the world. If this has already begun for you describe it to your group or in your journal.

2. What role has suffering played in your life?

3. In what ways do you feel you have actually "suffered for Christ"? Pray for others who are suffering for him now.

4. The story is told that one Christmas William Booth had a burning desire to communicate a greeting of encouragement to all Salvation Army citadels world-wide. They were going through a trying time, especially in the area of finances, and so he consulted with his aide.

His aide came back to him later with the news that it *was* possible to send a telegram to every citadel in the world, but the actual message could only be one word. The general retired for prayer and much later came back from his time of intercession with the Lord with the "one" word to send: Others!

Make one more poster for yourself. Place the word "others" in the center of it and place it where you will see it regularly.

Living in Style—One Word Follows Another

1. The list of the traits of the nature of Jesus is a lens through which we can view all of life, including scripture. Try another applicational Bible study, Matthew 18:21–35, remembering to ask three questions: A. What does this passage tell me about God? B. What does this tell me about myself? C. What does this tell me to do? Now, take the traits of Jesus and see if any of your answers to those three questions do not fit with those traits. Remember that the written Word must not violate the living Word. If, as you study scripture, you find areas that seem to violate Jesus, remember the Word is valid. This apparent incongruity simply means we must study more closely to learn how a specific passage does fulfill his nature.

2. Take the time to study the references about Jesus in the Old Testament. What do you suppose Jesus said to the two men on the road to Emmaus in Luke 24:13–27?

3. See how many places you can find where Jesus quoted the Old Testament.

4. Now that you are familiar with the traits of the nature of Jesus, as you read the New Testament, jot down the traits you see expressed in each passage.

Living in Style—The Style for All Seasons

1. Now that we have come to the last chapter, describe the changes of thought and action that have come to you while studying this book.

2. How do you feel about yourself now in relation to the list of the traits of Jesus? Does it seem overpowering?

3. In what ways are you seeing the role of the Holy Spirit in your life after this intense study of Jesus?

4. What ministries are you now planning? What new ways to give yourself away are lodged in your mind?

5. Read aloud the last two pages of the book beginning with the scripture verses from Philippians and Ephesians. What hope does this give you?

6. Read aloud Jude verses 24 and 25 and celebrate your "rest" in Jesus.

Gayle Erwin has spent thirty years as a pastor, college teacher, and magazine creator and editor. He devotes his time now to teaching and writing about the nature of Jesus.